Basic Collection of Children's Books in Spanish

by
ISABEL SCHON

The Scarecrow Press, Inc.
Metuchen, N.J., & London
1986

OTHER SCARECROW TITLES BY ISABEL SCHON:

A Bicultural Heritage

Books in Spanish for Children and Young Adults

Books in Spanish for Children and Young Adults, Series II

Books in Spanish for Children and Young Adults, Series III

A Hispanic Heritage

A Hispanic Heritage, Series II

Library of Congress Cataloging-in-Publication Data

Schon, Isabel.
    Basic collection of children's books in Spanish.

    Includes indexes.
    1. Children's literature, Spanish--Bibliography.
I. Title.
Z1037.7.S358   1986   016.86'0809282   86-13911
[PQ6168]
ISBN 0-8108-1904-X

To my parents,
Dr. Oswald Schon
and
Mrs. Anita Schon

to my husband,
Dr. Richard R. Chalquest

to my daughter,
Verita

• CONTENTS

• ACKNOWLEDGMENTS

Many people assisted in the preparation of this work. I would like to acknowledge especially the collaboration of Sarah Berman, Library Resource Specialist, Tempe Elementary School District #3, Tempe, Arizona, who classified all the materials and worked with me on the organization of this book.

I am also indebted to countless school and public librarians in Mexico, Spain, South America, California, and Arizona for their excellent suggestions; to the professional staffs of the University Library at Arizona State University, Phoenix Public Library, and San Diego Public Library for their invaluable assistance; and to Mrs. Eleanor Crabtree, Mrs. Aurelia García, Mrs. Hilda Loayza, and Mrs. Marjorie Woodruff for their kind cooperation.

Isabel Schon
Arizona State University, Tempe
March 1986

- INTRODUCTION

PURPOSE

Basic Collection of Children's Books in Spanish, whether used
for the development and support of an existing library collection or for the creation of a new library serving Spanish-
speaking children, recommends books in Spanish of high quality for inclusion in school or public libraries in the United
States or in any Spanish-speaking country. These books are
intended to support the informational, recreational and personal needs of Spanish-speaking children from preschool
through the sixth grade, although many of the books can also
be used by older students.

ARRANGEMENT AND USE

This book is arranged in the following sections: Reference
books; Nonfiction books, classified by the 11th Abridged Edition of the Dewey Decimal Classification in numerical order
from 000 to 999; Publishers' series, arranged alphabetically
by series title (individual titles are classed in the appropriate
Dewey number in Section II); Fiction; Easy books; and Professional books. Completing the volume is an appendix of
dealers of books in Spanish, followed by author, title, and
subject indexes.

Each book is listed under its main entry, which is us-
ually the author. For some books, however, the main entry
is under the title or series title.

To assist the non-Spanish-speaking selector, I have
translated each title into English and provided an extensive
annotation. Also, I have indicated a tentative grade level

for each book, but the individual student's Spanish reading ability, interest, taste, and purpose should be the main criteria for determining the true level of each book. In addition, I have provided a price for each book. It is important to realize, however, that prices of books in Spanish will definitely vary with dealer and time of purchase.

Most of the books reviewed were still in print as of March 1986. Unfortunately, however, as any experienced librarian knows, it is impossible to determine with any degree of certainty the availability of children's books in Spanish. Selectors are encouraged to check with various dealers (in the U.S. and abroad) before assuming that a book is out of print.

The selector will note that most of the books were published in Spain, Mexico, Argentina, and the United States. These countries are now publishing the best children's books in Spanish; other Spanish-speaking countries, unfortunately, still insist on moralizing to young readers or are too poor to offer an adequate selection of books to their young population.

Selectors will undoubtedly discover some gaps in this basic collection of children's books in Spanish. Omission of some important topics is due to unavailability, nonexistence at the time of compilation, or by my own lack of awareness.

• SECTION I: REFERENCE

Ref 030 GENERAL ENCYCLOPEDIC WORKS

Almanaque mundial 1986 [World Almanac 1986]. Virginia Gar-
dens, Fla.: Editorial América, 1985. 560p. ISBN Unavailable. $6. Gr. 5-Adult.
   An annual, general compendium of information related to
world events, scientific advances, sports news, world
economy, and the arts as well as population and economic
data on all countries.

Diccionario enciclopédico Espasa. Segunda Edición [Encyclopedic
Dictionary Espasa. Second Edition]. Madrid: Espasa-Calpe,
1985. 1,675p. ISBN 84-239-5913-9. $70. Gr. 6-adult.
   Photographs, maps, and diagrams in color and black
and white make this encyclopedic dictionary an attractive
quick-reference tool. It includes entries on various fields
of knowledge, such as geography, history, literature, the
arts, sciences, biography, and linguistics.

Enciclopedia Barsa [Encyclopedia Barsa]. 16 vols. Prepared
under the supervision of the Editors of Encyclopaedia Britannica. Mexico: Encyclopaedia Britannica de México, 1985.
ISBN 968-457-034-1. $699. Gr. 6-Adult.
   Easy-to-use encyclopedia with up-to-date entries and
specific, as well as general, information about the world.
In addition, it includes informative material on themes of
interest to the Hispanic world. Numerous black-and-white
and some color illustrations are also included.

Guinness libro de los records [Guinness Book of Records].

2   Basic Collection of Books in Spanish

Translated by Consuelo Reyes Torrent and Domingo Calde-
rilla. Madrid: Ediciones Maeva, 1985. 352p. ISBN 84-
86478-00-6. $22. Gr. 5-Adult.
   Spanish translation of this well-known collection of facts
about the natural world, animal kingdom, outer space, science, arts, technology, sports, and other fields wherever
records can be measured and broken.

Juego y me divierto [Never a Dull Moment]. Translated by
José María Pérez Miguel. Madrid: Editorial Everest, 1983.
93p. ISBN 84-241-5321-9. $8.95. Gr. 5-8.
   More than 40 different themes are discussed in two pages
each. It tells about dinosaurs, clouds, our solar system,
and rare plants, as well as magic, mime, masks, animated
cartoons, making three-dimensional objects, and other topics of interest to children. These are entertaining ideas
for a rainy day with simple, easy-to-follow illustrations.

Larsson, Lars Gunnar. Mini-Media, Enciclopedia Infantil
[Mini-Media Children's Encyclopedia]. 4 vols. Illustrated
by Tord Nyren. Translated from the Swedish by Rafael
Lassaletta. Madrid: Edaf Ediciones, 1985. ISBN 84-7166-
907-2. $80. Gr. 3-5.
   Especially designed for children, this encyclopedia includes 2,500 entries in Spanish, their English translations,
definitions, and numerous diagrams, illustrations, and photographs in color.

Loippe, Ulla. Lo que los niños quieren saber [What Children
Wish to Know]. Illustrated by Hannes Limmer. Madrid:
Editorial Everest, 1980. 280p. ISBN 84-241-5501-7. $26.
Gr. 4-6.
   This book answers questions commonly asked by children. Thus, it includes simple discussions with numerous
colorful illustrations on such topics as spaceships, the
weather, a car factory, a modern city, traffic regulations,
sports, and others. A well-designed index assists children
in locating specific topics.

Manley, Deborah. Es divertido descubrir cosas [It Is Fun to
Discover Things]. Illustrated by Moira and Colin Maclean

I. Reference   3

and Kailer-Lowndes. Translated by José Ferrer Aleu.
Barcelona: Plaza and Janes, S. A., 1981. 63p. ISBN
84-01-70097-3. $6. Gr. 4-7.
Basic facts about the world we live in, how people dress,
animals, weather, transportation, plants, nutrition, sounds,
and many other aspects of life are introduced to young
readers through brief descriptions and simple illustrations.

El niño pregunta: 9. Los animales del zoo; los árboles [A
Child Asks: Zoo Animals; Trees]. ISBN Unavailable.

El niño pregunta: 10. Las carreras de coches, La fuerza de
la naturaleza [A Child Asks: Auto Races; The Forces of
Nature]. ISBN 84-310-2774-6.

Ea. vol.: 61p. Translated from the German by Mariano y Rafael Orta. Color Photographs. Barcelona: Ediciones Toray, 1983. $4.75. Gr. 5-9.
Like their predecessors, the two new titles in this series are simply written with excellent color photographs.
They describe basic facts about zoo animals, trees, auto
races, and the forces of nature. They include answers to
simple questions, such as, Is the tiger dangerous? What
is the difference between the leopard and the panther?
How does a tree know that it is spring? How much gaso-
line does a race car need? What is a volcano?

Ref 220.9 GEOGRAPHY, HISTORY, CHRONOLOGY,
PERSONS OF BIBLE LANDS IN BIBLE TIMES
(including Bible stories retold)

Marshall-Taylor, Geoffrey (Adapted by). La Biblia ilustrada
para niños [The Illustrated Children's Bible]. Illustrated
by Andrew Aloof and others. Translated from the English
by Rafael Lassaletta. Madrid: Edaf Ediciones, 1981. 255p.
ISBN 84-7166-748-7. $20. Gr. 4-9.
The times and stories of the Old and New Testaments
are exquisitely introduced to children in an easy flowing
text and with spectacular illustrations in color.

Ref 463 SPANISH LANGUAGE DICTIONARIES

A Child's Picture Dictionary English/Spanish. Illustrated by

Dennis Sheheen. New York: Adama Books, 1984. 44p.
ISBN 0-915361-11-6. $8. Gr. PK-2.
    The simple ABC includes outstanding illustrations ac-
companying each letter of the alphabet. In addition, each
English word includes a Spanish translation. The ever-
increasing demand for bilingual books should make this one
a favorite of parents, teachers, and children. It should
be noted, however, that this is not a bilingual picture dictionary, but rather an English ABC with Spanish translations.

Diccionario Temático: Sinónimos y Antónimos [Thematic Dictionary: Synonyms and Antonyms]. Madrid: Editorial
Everest, 1983. 638p. ISBN 84-241-1501-5. $10. Gr. 6-
adult.
    Excellent dictionary which gives meanings, usage notes,
synonyms, and antonyms in Spanish.

González, Mike. Collins Concise Spanish-English English-
Spanish Dictionary. New York: Simon and Schuster,
1985. 1,024p. ISBN 0-671-60469-4. $16.95. Gr. 5-
adult.
    Good, basic bilingual Spanish-English and English-
Spanish dictionary with over 100,000 references which can
be easily used by students or teachers. Most frequently
used words in both languages are treated in detail, and
numerous phrases and examples show how particular words
are used in different contexts.

Mi primer Sopena: diccionario infantil ilustrado [My First
Sopena: Illustrated Children's Dictionary]. Illustrated
by Carlos Busquets. Barcelona: Editorial Ramón Sopena,
1967. 130p. ISBN 84-303-0064-3. $13. Gr. 3-6.
    Simple Spanish dictionary with 1,000 definitions and
700 illustrations which should assist young Spanish readers
in learning how to use a dictionary. Each entry gives the
grammatical usage of the word as well as illustrative words
and sentences.

Sopena Inglés de los niños: diccionario infantil ilustrado,
Español-Inglés [Sopena English for Children: Illustrated

Children's Dictionary]. Barcelona: Editorial Ramón Sopena,
1983. 63p. ISBN 84-303-0893-8. $8. Gr. 3-6.
Basic bilingual (Spanish-English only) dictionary which
includes 1,000 entries and 350 illustrations. Each Spanish
word is accompanied by its English translation and is used
in a sentence in both languages.

Zendrera, Concepción, and Noelle Granger. Mi primer diccionario ilustrado [My First Illustrated Dictionary]. Barcelona: Editorial Juventud, 1984. 24p. ISBN 84-261-
0358-8. $7. Gr. K-3.
One hundred and forty-eight Spanish words are included
in this delightful dictionary for young children. Simple,
colorful illustrations and an easy-to-understand sentence
explain the meaning of each word. This is an excellent
introduction to the Spanish alphabet for young children.

Ref 501.4 SCIENCE LANGUAGES (TERMINOLOGY),
COMMUNICATION

Godman, Arthur. Diccionario ilustrado de las ciencias [Long-
man Illustrated Science Dictionary]. Translated by Pilar
Pérez Valdelomar and Julio Herrero. Madrid: Editorial
Everest, 1984. 278p. ISBN 84-241-1520-1. $10. Gr. 6-
adult.
A compact yet comprehensive science dictionary which
includes 1,500 basic scientific words divided in three
principal groups: physics, chemistry, and biology. One
third of the space is given to diagrams and illustrations
in color. It also includes Spanish-English and English-
Spanish translations. Definitely a useful, quick reference
for teachers and able students.

Ref 709 HISTORICAL AND GEOGRAPHIC TREATMENT OF
FINE AND DECORATIVE ARTS

Javier, Carlos, and Taranilla de la Varga. Diccionario temático
de historia del arte [Thematic Dictionary of Art History].
Madrid: Editorial Everest, 1983. 510p. ISBN 84-241-
1506-6. $14. Gr. 6-adult.
A concise dictionary of art history written for the lay-
person with numerous color and black-and-white photo-

graphs and drawings. It is especially good in European
art.

Ref 912 GRAPHIC REPRESENTATIONS OF
SURFACE OF EARTH

Olliver, Jane. Atlas Molino Ilustrado [Molino Illustrated At-
las]. Barcelona: Editorial Molino, 1979. 61p. ISBN 84-
272-5938-7. $16. Gr. 4-8.
   Colorful atlas which begins with the Earth in space, followed by sections that describe the Earth, Europe, Asia,
Africa, America, and Oceania.

Tivers, Jacqueline, and Michael Day. Atlas infantil Everest
[Everest Children's Atlas]. Madrid: Editorial Everest,
1983. 47p. ISBN 84-241-6097-5. $7. Gr. 3-5.
   Most appealing atlas for young children, with attractive
illustrations, maps, and photographs in color. It includes
a few short paragraphs about each continent or country
in the world. This is not a comprehensive atlas, but
rather an introduction to the countries of the world.

• SECTION II: NONFICTION

004 DATA PROCESSING. COMPUTER SCIENCE

Bramhill, Peter. El mundo de la computadora [The World of
Computers]. Illustrated by Graham Smith. Translated by
Liliana Vogelbaum. Buenos Aires: Editorial Sigmar, 1984.
61p. ISBN 950-11-0369-2. $10.95. Gr. 6-12.
Numerous illustrations in color and a direct, easy-to-
understand text introduce readers to the world of computers. It explains the various uses of computers, how
they work, and how they may be used in the future.

Graham, Ian. El Ordenador [Computer]. Barcelona: Mar-
combo Boixareu Editores, 1984. 37p. Biblioteca Técnica
Juvenil. ISBN 84-267-0521-9. $8.95. Gr. 6-10.
For full annotation, see series title in Section III.

Novelli, Luca. Mi primer libro sobre ordenadores [My First
Book About Computers]. Translated from the Italian by
José Golacheca. Madrid: Ediciones Generales Anaya, 1983.
64p. ISBN 84-7525-144-7. $8.50. Gr. 5-10.
This is a basic introduction to computers in a witty,
easy-to-read, comic-book style. It includes the early and
modern history of computers, how they are made, what they
can do, how they can be programmed, and their uses at
work, at school, and for recreational purposes. Amusing
introduction to a popular topic.

005.1 COMPUTER PROGRAMMING

Novelli, Luca. Mi primer libro de Basic [My First Book About

7

8 Basic Collection of Books in Spanish

Basic]. Translated from the Italian by José Golacheca.
Madrid: Ediciones Generales Anaya, 1984. 64p. ISBN 84-
7525-175-7. $9. Gr. 6-10.
Like the previous book by this author, which introduced computers to young readers, this book is a witty,
simple explanation of the elementary concepts of the computer language, Basic. It teaches the reader to write
very simple programs. Comic-book style illustrations explain the common words required to write a simple program
in Basic.

Smith, Brian Reffin. Programación de computadoras [Com-
puter Programming]. Madrid: Ediciones Plesa, 1983.
48p. Colección Electrónica. ISBN Unavailable. $3.95.
Gr. 5-10.
For full annotation, see series title in Section III.

Watt, Sofía, and Miguel Mangada. Basic para niños [Basic
for Children]. Madrid: Paraninfo, 1984. 128p. ISBN
84-283-1327-x. $8.95. Gr. 6-12.
Fundamental concepts of programming in Basic are explained to young readers. It also includes simple notes to
parents or educators to assist young readers in further
understanding Basic. It concludes with a few brief programs that young readers can enter into and play on a
computer.

128 HUMANKIND--LIFE, DEATH, SOUL, MIND

Mellonie, Bryan, and Robert Ingpen. Principio y fin: ciclo
de vida que transcurre entre el nacer y el morir [Begin-
nings and Endings with Lifetimes in Between]. Translated by Carmen Esteva and Miguel Leon Garza. México:
Compañía Editorial Continental, 1984. [40p.] ISBN 968-
26-0514-8. $5. Gr. 3-5.
As a basic introduction for young readers to the cycle
of life, this book does serve a purpose. Through outstanding color illustrations and a simple text, it tells that
for all plants, people, birds, fish, trees, and animals there
is a beginning and an end.

152.4 EMOTIONS AND FEELINGS

Simon, Norma. Cuando me enojo [I Was So Mad]. Illustrated
by Dora Leder. Translated by Alma Flor Ada. Chicago:
Albert Whitman and Co., 1976. 40p. ISBN 0-8075-9429-6.
$10.25. Gr. 3-5.
   This is an excellent translation of Simon's I Was So Mad.
Young readers should relate to many situations depicted in
this book in which children naturally react in anger. Feelings of frustration, anxiety, humiliation, and loss of control
are portrayed. The basic messages are "Everybody gets
mad sometimes," and "It's not bad to be angry--once in a
while." Lively, three-tone illustrations complement each
scene.

220.9 GEOGRAPHY, HISTORY, CHRONOLOGY, PERSONS
OF BIBLE LANDS IN THE BIBLE TIMES

Cichello, Rubén D., and Clara Inés Fernández. Papa Noel
y la historia de navidad [Father Noel and the Christmas
Story]. Buenos Aires: Ediciones Paulinas, 1984. 32p.
ISBN 950-09-0471-3. $3.50. Gr. 3-6.
   In a light-hearted, poetic style, Father Noel narrates
the story of the birth of Christ. Vivacious watercolor illustrations add a festive touch to this gay Christmas poem.

Manley, Deborah. Es divertido descubrir la época de la biblia.
[It Is Fun to Discover the Bible's Era]. Illustrated by
Moira and Colin Maclean. Barcelona: Plaza y Janés, 1983.
47p. ISBN 84-01-70183-X. $6. Gr. 5-8.
   Through busy, colorful illustrations and a brief text,
young readers are introduced to the Bible. Manley tells
about the people and places that were important at the
time the Bible was written, as well as Jesus' early life and
works.

232.91 MARY, MOTHER OF JESUS (MARIOLOGY)
(including annunciation, miracles, apparitions)

De Paola, Tomie. Nuestra Señora de Guadalupe [The Lady
of Guadalupe]. Illustrated by the author. Translated by
Pura Belpré. New York: Holiday House, 1980. [48p.]
ISBN 0-8234-0374-2. $10.95. Gr. K-3.

This is an excellent Spanish translation of The Lady of
Guadalupe. Striking color illustrations and a well-written
text tell the story of Mexico's patron saint, the Lady of
Guadalupe, who appeared to a poor Mexican Indian, Juan
Diego, in 1531. Young readers will be delighted by this
re-creation of the legend of the beautiful lady who, in the
robes of an Aztec princess, asked Juan Diego to tell the
Bishop in Mexico City to build a church in her honor on
the hill where she was standing.

291.1 COMPARATIVE RELIGION, MYTHOLOGY AND MYTHOLOGICAL FOUNDATIONS

Al-Saleh, Jairat. Ciudades fabulosas, príncipes y yinn de la
mitología árabe [Fabled Cities, Princes and Jinn from
Arab Myths and Legends]. Illustrated by Rashad N.
Salim. 132 p. ISBN 84-7525-290-7.

Branston, Brian. Dioses y héroes de la mitología vikinga
[Gods and Heroes from Viking Mythology]. Illustrated by
Giovanni Caselli. 156p. ISBN 84-7525-237-0.

Gibson, Michael. Monstruos, dioses y hombres de la mitología
griega [Gods, Men and Monsters from the Greek Myths].
Illustrated by Giovanni Caselli. 156p. ISBN 84-7525-190-0.

Usher, Kerry. Emperadores, dioses y héroes de la mitología
romana [Heroes, Gods and Emperors from Roman Mythol-
ogy]. Illustrated by John Sibbick. 132p. ISBN 84-7525-
189-7.

Ea. vol. (Mitología). Madrid: Ediciones Generales
Anaya, 1985. $17. Gr. 6-12.
This spectacular series on mythology of the world will
entice all readers. Each volume includes dazzling illustrations in color and black and white as well as a flowing
text. Previous titles in this series are Guerreros, dioses
y espíritus de la mitología de América Central y Sudamérica [Warriors, Gods and Spirits of the Mythology of Central
and South America] by Douglas Gifford, and Dragones,
dioses y espíritus de la mitología china [Dragons, Gods
and Spirits of Chinese Mythology] by Tao Tao Liu Sanders.

307.7 SPECIFIC KINDS OF COMMUNITIES
(Rural, Suburban, Urban)

Solano Flores, Guillermo. La calle [The Street]. Illustrated
by Gloria Calderas Lim. México: Editorial Trillas, 1986.
16p. ISBN 968-24-1780-5. $3. Gr. 2-4.
Describes various activities taking place on city streets.
For full entry, see series title, Ojos abiertos, in Section
III.

Solano Flores, Guillermo. El campo [The Countryside]. Illus-
trated by Silvia Luz Alvarado. México: Editorial Trillas,
1986. 16p. ISBN 968-24-1779-1. $3. Gr. 2-4.
Tells about life in the country among trees and animals.
For full entry, see series title, Ojos abiertos, in Section
III.

331.7 LABOR BY INDUSTRY AND OCCUPATION

Neigoff, Anne. Cuando trabaja la gente [When People Work].

_____. Donde trabaja la gente [Where People Work].

_____. Porqué trabaja la gente [Why People Work].

_____. Qué trabajo puedes hacer [Work You Can Do].

_____. Quién trabaja [Who Works].

Ea. vol.: Illustrated by Phil Renaud. Translated by
International Language Communications Center. (Ahora
Sabes Sobre la Gente en el Trabajo). Chicago: Encyclopaedia Britannica Educational Corporation, 1974. 32p.
ISBN 0-87827-190-2. $99. Gr. 4-6.
Excellent Spanish translation of the series "Now You
Know About People at Work," which offers children many
opportunities "to observe or compare a wide variety of
career areas and to discover that there are many different
kinds of workers and that each worker contributes to our
daily needs." A Teacher's Guide written in English suggests other learning activities. Cuando trabaja la gente
explains that people work in a variety of time sequences
to provide our daily needs. Donde trabaja la gente ex-

plains that people work in a wide variety of places and
that in almost every place in the world someone is working.
Porqué trabaja la gente tells that people work to provide
for their own needs and to provide for the needs of other
people. Qué trabajo puedes hacer helps children to become aware of the wide range of career choices that lie
ahead of them. Quién trabaja introduces children to a
wide variety of career areas and to the concept that each
career area is important to our daily lives. Each book has
a correlated cassette.

333.91 UTILIZATION OF OTHER NATURAL RESOURCES
(Water and Land Adjoining It)

Giron, Nicole. El agua [The Water]. Illustrated by Felipe
Morales. México: Editorial Patria, 1981. 36p. ISBN 96-
839-0002-X. $4. Gr. 3-5.
   The importance of water in rural Mexico is depicted
through a simple text and colorful illustrations. It emphasizes the significance of conserving water and of using
water for farming, for producing electricity, and for bathing and washing. Some readers might object to two scenes:
a nude woman bathing in a river and a nude boy fishing
for carp.

363.2 POLICE SERVICES

Broekel, Ray. La policía [Police]. Translated by Lada Kratky. Chicago: Childrens Press, 1984. 48p. ISBN 0-516-
31643-5. $8.95. Gr. 2-4.
   Full annotation under series title, Así es mi mundo, in
Section III. Photos, drawings, index.

363.3 ASPECTS OF PUBLIC SAFETY

Usborne, Peter, and Su Swallow. Fuego [Fire]. Barcelona:
Editorial Molino, 1981. 24p. ISBN 84-272-5002-9. $3.
Gr. 1-3.
   For full entry see series title, Biblioteca Educativa In-
fantil Molino, in Section III.

380.5 TRANSPORTATION

El transporte [Transportation]. Barcelona: Afha Internacional, 1979. 52p. ISBN Unavailable. $6. Gr. 5-8.
For full entry see series title, El hombre y su entorno,
in Section III.

385 RAILROAD TRANSPORTATION

Usborne, Peter, and Su Swallow. Trenes [Trains]. Barcelona: Editorial Molino, 1981. 24p. ISBN 84-272-5013-4.
$3. Gr. 1-3.
For full entry see series title, Biblioteca educativa infantil Molino, in Section III.

387.5023 OCEAN (MARINE) TRANSPORTATION AS PROFESSION, OCCUPATION, HOBBY

Grée, Alain. Yo quiero ser capitán [I Want to Be a Captain].
Buenos Aires: Editorial Sigmar, 1973. 12p. ISBN Un-
available. $3. Gr. 3-6.
Through the eyes of a young captain, the reader is
introduced to different kinds of ships, such as caravels,
Viking, pirate, freight, passenger, and fishing boats.
The simple descriptions and attractive illustrations make
this an appealing story for young readers.

Puncel, María. Cuando sea mayor seré marino [When I'm
Older, I Will Be a Seaman]. Illustrated by Ulises Wensel.
Madrid: Ediciones Altea, 1980. 44p. ISBN 84-372-1388-
5. $5. Gr. 5-8.
Through the eyes of a boy approximately twelve-years-
old, young readers are exposed to the life of a seaman.
It describes many duties that must be performed to keep
a boat in good condition, as well as the comforts and problems of life at sea. It emphasizes the education and preparation necessary to become an expert and the various types
of boats that are available. There is action and excitement
in this introduction to seafaring. Colorful illustrations
complement each page.

388.4 LOCAL TRANSPORTATION

Grée, Alain. Tom e Irene y el código de circulación [Tom and Irene and Traffic Regulations]. Illustrated by Gerard Grée. Barcelona: Editorial Juventud, 1981. 21p. ISBN 84-261-5748-3. $3. Gr. 4-6.
Uncle Nicolás explains to Tom and Irene the need for traffic regulations. He tells them about safety belts, safe driving, traffic signs, and safe pedestrian habits. Simple illustrations complement the text.

391 COSTUME AND DRESS

Usborne, Peter, and Su Swallow. Vestidos [Dress]. Barcelona: Editorial Molino, 1981. 24p. ISBN 84-272-5017-7. $3. Gr. 1-3.
For full entry see series title, Biblioteca Educativa Infantil Molino, in Section III.

394.2 GENERAL CUSTOMS, SPECIAL OCCASIONS

Gorostiza, Carlos. Los días de fiesta [Holidays]. Illustrated by Blanca Medda. Buenos Aires: Editorial Kapelusz, 1978. 14p. ISBN Unavailable. $3. Gr. 1-3.
Various holidays well known to Hispanic children are depicted through attractive illustrations and simple rhymes. It includes New Year's Eve, the Three Wise Men, carnivals, national holidays, birthdays, Columbus Day, and Christmas.

398 FOLKLORE

Bayley, Nicola. Canciones tontas [Silly Songs]. Translated by Javier Roca. Barcelona: Editorial Lumen, 1982. [32p.] ISBN 84-264-3566-1. $4.50. Gr. 2-5.
These are well-done translations of some popular and some lesser-known English nursery rhymes. It includes "Humpty Dumpty," "This Little Pig Went to Market," "There Was an Old Woman Who Lived in a Shoe," and others. Attractive, colorful illustrations complement each rhyme. Unfortunately, the rhymes lack titles, and the book does not have an index or a table of contents.

Bravo-Villasante, Carmen. Advina adivinanza. Folklore infantil [Riddles, Children's Folklore]. Madrid: Interduc/
Schroedel, 1979. 80p. ISBN 84-388-0651-1. $9. Gr. K-
5.
   This is an amusing collection of traditional riddles,
tongue-twisters, singing games, nursery rhymes, Christmas carols, and prayers that are well known in Spanish-
speaking countries. The brevity and sense of word play
inherent in the Hispanic oral tradition are beautifully maintained for children. The illustrations are nineteenth-
century lithographs in color. Some are quite charming;
others are a little too cute.

Bravo-Villasante, Carmen. Arre moto piti, poto, arre, moto,
piti, pa [Arre, moto, piti, poto, arre, moto, piti, pa].
Illustrated by Juan Romero. Madrid: Editorial Escuela
Española, 1984. 46p. ISBN 84-331-0269-0. $4.95. Gr.
3-5.
   Wide diversity of nursery rhymes, tongue twisters,
games, and Christmas carols are included in this paperback
publication with decorative two-tone illustrations. Some of
the selections are well-known favorites; others are region-
al versions.

Bravo-Villasante, Carmen. China, China, Capuchina, en esta
mano está la china [China, china...]. Illustrated by Carmen Andrada. Valladolid: Miñón, 1981. 106p. ISBN 84-
355-0560-X. $9. Gr. PK-4.
   This is a delightful collection of traditional Hispanic
children's rhymes, riddles, games, and songs. Unfortunately, the black-and-white, undersized illustrations do not add
much excitement to these rhymes and games which, as this
well-known author states, are "alegría y poesía [happiness
and poetry]." Nevertheless, there is a wealth of joy in
their simplicity and charm so that young children will enjoy reading them or being read to.

Bravo-Villasante, Carmen. El libro de los 500 refranes
[Book of 500 Proverbs]. Illustrated by Carmen Andrada.
Valladolid: Editorial Miñón, 1981. 136p. ISBN 84-355-
0591-X. $8. Gr. 5-12.
   This is a delightful collection of 500 well-known Hispanic

16   Basic Collection of Books in Spanish

proverbs. The brevity of these proverbs as well as their
timeless quality should appeal to readers of all ages.
Bravo-Villasante states in the introduction that she selected these proverbs because "they are positive, optimis-
tic and hopeful, and they give good advice."

Fernández, Laura, ed. De tín marín: cantos y rondas infantiles [Miny Mo's: Children's Songs and Rhymes]. Illustrated by the editor. México: Editorial Trillas, 1983.
[16p.] ISBN 968-24-1469-5. $3. Gr. PK-2.
Seven well-known Mexican nursery rhymes with engaging watercolor illustrations are included in this publication: "Un elefante se balanceaba," "De tín, marín,"
"La gallina popujada," "Aquel caracol," "Conejo Blás,"
"Hojas de té," and "Papas para papá." These nursery
rhymes are sure to appeal to young children anywhere.
It does not include a table of contents or an index.

Fernández, Laura, ed. Pío Pío: cantos y rondas infantiles
[Pío Pío: Children's Songs and Rhymes]. Illustrated by
the editor. México: Editorial Trillas, 1983. [16p.]
ISBN 968-24-1470-9. $3. Gr. PK-2.
Three delightful Mexican nursery rhymes are included
in this attractive publication with striking watercolor il-
lustrations. It includes "Los pollitos dicen, 'Pío, Pío,
Pío,'" "Soy indita carbonera," and "Una rata vieja."

Griego, Margot C.; Betsy L. Bucks; Sharon S. Gilbert; and
Laurel H. Kimball. Tortillitas para Mamá and Other
Nursery Rhymes: Spanish and English. Illustrated by
Barbara Cooney. New York: Holt, Rinehart and Winston,
1981. [28p.] ISBN 0-03-056704-1. $9.95. Gr. PK-2.
This is a delightful bilingual collection of 13 well-known
Hispanic nursery rhymes which have been passed on to
each generation of Hispanic children. It includes such old-
time-favorites as "La Viejita" ("The Little Old Lady"), "Co-
lita de Rana" ("Little Frog Tail"), "Los Pollitos" ("The
Chicks"), and "Arrullo" ("Lullaby").
Barbara Cooney's undeniable artistic abilities add much
charm to each nursery rhyme. However, it is indeed re-
grettable that most of her illustrations depict the common,
stereotyped scenes of barefooted peasants in quaint, rural

settings. (Illustrators and editors should update their impressions of Hispanic people, both in the U.S. and abroad. Most Hispanic people live in urban settings.) Only two of the illustrations depict Hispanic people with a sincere warmth and understanding; illustrations like these two would have made this book of nursery rhymes a sure winner.

Ramírez, Elisa. Adivinanzas indígenas [Indigenous Riddles]. Illustrated by Máximo Javier. Mexico: Editorial Patria, 1984. 31p. ISBN Unavailable. $3. Gr. 1-3.
    For full entry see series title, Colección Piñata, in Section III.

Schon, Isabel, ed. Doña Blanca and Other Hispanic Nursery Rhymes and Games. Minneapolis, Minn.: T. S. Denison and Co., 1983. 41p. ISBN 513-01768-2. $7. Gr. K-6.
    Eighteen well-known Hispanic nursery rhymes and games are included in this bilingual (Spanish-English) publication. Two-tone illustrations and simple instructions explain to the reader how to play the games. Some of the rhymes and games included are "Riquirrán," "La Cucaracha," "Andale, Anita," "A la rueda de San Miguel," "A la Víbora," and "Matarile-Rile-Ró."

398.2 FOLK LITERATURE

Alegría, Ricardo E. Cuentos folklóricos de Puerto Rico [Folklore Stories of Puerto Rico]. Illustrated by Rafael Seco. Puerto Rico: Colección de Estudios Puertorriqueños, 1982. 120p. ISBN 84-399-0855-5. $11. Gr. 3-6.
    Twelve well-known Puerto Rican folktales written in simple language but unfortunately the illustrations are disfigured and blurred. Some outstanding titles are "Los tres hermanos y los objectos maravillosos: (p. 11), "Juan Bobo y la Princesa Adivinadora" (p. 31), "Juan Bobo, la puerca, los pollos y el caldero" (p. 69), and "Los tres deseos" (p. 25). The simple, fluid writing style of these tales makes them truly enjoyable reading.

Armellada, Fray Cesáreo de. El cocuyo y la mora [The Fire-

fly and the Mulberry]. Adapted by Kurusa and Verónica
Uribe. Illustrated by Amelie Areco. Caracas: Ediciones
Ekaré, 1978. [34p.] ISBN Unavailable. $5. Gr. 1-3.
This charming folktale from Venezuela tells why fireflies are now black and emit light from their tails. It also
explains that fireflies still court mulberry trees when they
are in bloom, as they are still waiting for their love.
Pleasing, colorful illustrations complement this entertaining
tale.

Armellada, Fray Cesáreo de. Panton ... (Una mano de cuentos
de los indios pemón) [Panton ... A story collection of the
Pemón Indians]. Caracas: Consucre, 1979. [54p.] ISBN
Unavailable. $5. Gr. 4-8.
Five beautiful legends of the Pemón Indians of Venezuela
have been collected and translated into Spanish by Armellada in this outstanding book with spectacular, colorful illustrations. It includes the following: "Un rayo trueno
herido," which gives a vision of beings that live in the
clouds: "Un indio se fue tras una venadita," which tells
how an Indian becomes a good hunter; "El indio ayudador
de una culebra," which criticizes an Indian who started a
fire without adequate precautions; "Un indio tragado por
una boa," which tells how a brave Indian freed himself
from a snake; and "El tigre inferior a la rana," which
shows how a tiger was defeated by a frog. The Pemón
version of these legends is also included.
Perhaps the only flaw in this otherwise excellent collection is that the text is printed in very small size, which
makes it hard to read.

Armellada, Fray Cesáreo de. El rabipelado burlado [The
Outwitted Porcupine]. Illustrated by Vicky Sempere.
Caracas: Ediciones Ekaré, 1978. 32p. ISBN Unavailable.
$5. Gr. 1-3.
This amusing legend from the Pemón tribe from the
Guayana del Sur region of Venezuela tells why porcupines
eat roots, fruits, and seeds. Lively animal illustrations
and a simple text describe hungry porcupine in his constant but unsuccessful search for food. A brief introduction tells about the Pemón people of Venezuela. Young
readers will need to be told that this tale uses the names
of the animals as they are known in Venezuela: "Rabipelado"

for porcupine, "Trompetero" for trumpeter, "Piapoco" for toucan, and "Poncha" for dove.

Armellada, Fray Cesáreo de. El tigre y el rayo. Cuento de la tribu pemón [The Tiger and Lightning. Story of the Pemón Tribe]. Adapted by Kurusa y Verónica Uribe. Illustrated by Aracelis Ocante. Caracas: Ediciones Ekaré-Banco del Libro, 1979. 22p. ISBN Unavailable. $3. Gr. 1-3.

The excellent adaptation of a Pemón legend from Venezuela tells how a vain jaguar (Venezuelan tiger) was humiliated by humble lightning. A simple and readable text makes this story delightful reading for young children as they follow the jaguar in his early attempts to impress lightning, and then see how lightning can easily frighten the jaguar wherever he goes. The jaguar admits defeat and goes home. Colorful, bold illustrations beautifully complement the text.

Basile, Giambattista. Petrosinella [Petrosinella]. Illustrated by Diane Stanley. Translated by Felipe Garrido. México: Promexa, 1982. 40p. ISBN 968-34-0178-3. $5. Gr. 4-8.

For full entry see series title, Clásicos infantiles ilustrados Promexa, in Section III.

Belpré, Pura. Oté [Ote]. Illustrated by Paul Galdone. New York: Pantheon Books, 1969. 28p. ISBN Unavailable. $5. Gr. 1-3.

Puerto Rican folktale narrated by the well-known Puerto Rican librarian Pura Belpré as she remembers it told by her grandfather. The tale describes a very poor family who did not have enough to eat. The father, Oté, found the near-sighted devil, who ended up eating most of the family's food. Oté would not follow the advice of the old woman and the family had to be saved by Chiquitín's courage.

Belpré, Pura. Pérez y Martina [Pérez and Martina]. Illustrated by Carlos Sánchez M. New York: Warne, 1961. 58p. ISBN Unavailable. $5. Gr. 1-3.

Entertaining version of the popular Puerto Rican folktale "Pérez y Martina," with attractive colorful illustrations written in simple language. The repetitive marriage proposals by diverse animals to the attractive and royal Spanish cockroach maiden will amuse children as well as the surprising ending in which the elegant mouse Perez falls to his death into a boiling bottle.

Berenguer, Carmen. El rey mocho [The King with the Missing Ear]. Adapted by Verónica Uribe. Illustrated by Luz María Hevia. Caracas: Ediciones Ekaré-Banco del Libro, 1981. [20p.] ISBN Unavailable. $3. Gr. 2-4.
    Latin American version of a popular folktale collected by the Grimm brothers which tells about a king who was missing one ear. When his old barber died, he swore the new barber to secrecy. It wasn't the barber but a sugar cane plant that gave away the king's secret. Colorful illustrations complement the simple text.

Cuentos picarescos para niños de América Latina [Picaresque Tales for Children from Latin America]. Caracas: Ekaré/ Banco del Libro, 1983. 80p. ISBN Unavailable. $5. Gr. 5-10.
    This collection of eight tales from Central and South America demonstrates the ingenuity of sharp-witted trickster heroes who survive due to their own cunningness and resourcefulness. Pedro Malasartes from Brazil, Domingo Siete from Colombia, Tío Conejo from Ecuador and Nicaragua, Pedro Urdemales from Guatemala, Casimiro from Peru, Juan Bobo from the Dominican Republic, and Pedro Rimales from Venezuela prove that you do not need wealth or power to triumph in this world. Cheerful watercolor illustrations complement these amusing folktales.

Cuentos rusos [Russian Stories]. Illustrated by Ivan Yakovlevich Bilibin. Barcelona: Editorial Lumen, 1981. 47p. ISBN 84-264-3568-8. $6. Gr. 6-9.
    Collection of three traditional Russian tales that tell about beautiful maidens, courageous young men, wicked witches, and helpful old ladies. The exquisite illustrations of Russian scenes and the inherent appeal of these time-honored tales make them an enjoyable introduction to the study of Russia and its people.

Esopo. El Zorro que perdió la cola [The Fox Who Lost His
Tail]. Illustrated by Bennett. Translated by Ana María
Matute. Barcelona: Instituto Parramón Ediciones, 1979.
[36p.] ISBN 84-342-0169-0. $5. Gr. 5-8.
  Seventeen brief fables with their appropriate morals
and charming illustrations tell about a fox that lost its
tail, a wolf and a lamb, a crab and its mother, a monkey
and her children, a lion and a mosquito, and others.

Ferré, Rosario. Los cuentos de Juan Bobo [Stories of Juan
the Fool]. Illustrated by José Rosa. Río Piedras: Ediciones Huracán, Inc., 1981. 31p. ISBN 0-940238-62-4.
$5. Gr. 6-12.
  Five delightful stories about "Juan, the Fool" are included in this unpretentious publication with two-tone
woodcut illustrations. They tell about Juan and the young
ladies of Manto Prieto, Juan going to mass, Juan dining at
a wealthy home, Juan staying at home, and Juan going to
the capital. The simplicity and witticism of these stories
should captivate most readers.

Galeano, Eduardo. Aventuras de los jóvenes dioses [Adven-
tures of the Young Gods]. Illustrated by Delia Contarbio.
Buenos Aires: Editorial Kapelusz, 1984. 32p. ISBN 950-
13-5357-5. $4. Gr. 5-9.
  The adventures of two young gods, Hunahpú and his
brother Ixbalanqué, who came to earth to destroy the Kingdom of Fear, are narrated in a fast-moving pace. Colorful pre-Columbian-style illustrations complement the story
of the victorious gods--Hunahpú, who is now the sun of
every day, and Ixbalanqué, the moon of every night.

Garrido, Felipe. Tajín y los sietes truenos [Tajin and the
Seven Thunderbolts]. Illustrated by Pedro Bayona.
México: Promexa, 1982. 40p. ISBN 968-34-0170-8. $5.
Gr. 4-8.
  For full entry see series title, Clásicos infantiles ilustra-
dos Promexa, in Section III.

Garrido de Rodríquez, Neli. Leyendas argentinas [Argentinian
Legends]. Illustrated by José Miguel Heredia. Buenos

Aires: Editorial Plus Ultra, 1981. 111p. ISBN Unavailable. $11. Gr. 6-10.
Delightful collection of 19 pre-Columbian legends from South America that are simply written. They tell of how violence between two tribes was turned into friendship thanks to Onagait's beautiful messenger, the punishment of the treacherous "Curupí," the love between a graceful princess and a valiant warrior, a little girl who made rain, and other entertaining legends.
The fast-pace and alluring characters make these legends a charming introduction to the people and natural resources of South America. The only unappealing parts of this book are the awkward two-tone illustrations.

Goble, Paul. El don del perro sagrado [The Gift of the Sacred Dog]. Illustrated by the author. Translated by Felipe Garrido. México: Promexa, 1982. 40p. ISBN 968-34-0166-X. $5. Gr. 4-8.
For full entry see series title, Clásicos infantiles ilustrados Promexa, in Section III.

Grimm, Hermanos. Blanca nieves y los siete enanos [Snow-White and the Seven Dwarfs]. Illustrated by Nancy Ekholm Burkert. Spanish version: Felipe Garrido. México: Promociones Editoriales Mexicanas, 1982. [30p.] ISBN 968-34-0163-5. $5. Gr. 4-6.
Good translation of Snow-White and the Seven Dwarfs with striking illustrations.

Grimm, Jacob. La bella durmiente [Thorn Rose--Sleeping Beauty]. Illustrated by Errol Le Cain. Translated by José Emilio Pacheco. México: Promexa, 1982. 40p. ISBN 968-34-0164-3. $5. Gr. 4-8.
For full entry see series title, Clásicos infantiles ilustrados Promexa, in Section III.

Grimm, Jacob. Cuentos de Grimm [Grimm's Stories]. #8. Madrid: Ediciones Auriga, 1984. 16p. ISBN 84-7281-152-4. $2.95. Gr. 5-8.
Series title: Cuentos de siempre [Stories for Always].
Includes such stories as "Los músicos de la ciudad de

Bremen" ["Bremen Town Musicians"], "Historia del hombre
que no tenía miedo" ["The Man of Iron"], and "El Pescador
y su mujer" ["Fisherman and His Wife"] written in a fast-
moving text with delightful pastel illustrations.

Grimm, Jacob. A pillo, pillo y medio [A Rogue and a Half].
Illustrated by Beat Brusch. Translated by Ana María
Matute. Barcelona: Instituto Parramón Ediciones, 1979.
[20p.] ISBN 84-342-0172-0. $4. Gr. 3-5.
    The story of a hard-working farmer that knew how to
deal with the devil and at the same time acquire the devil's
treasure is simply told. Young readers will delight in the
farmer's ingenuity and in the attractive illustrations.

Guait, Camilo. La fantástica historia de Jimmy Button [Jimmy
Button's Fantastic Story]. Illustrated by Blas Alfredo
Castagna. Buenos Aires: Ediciones Toqui, 1977. 46p.
ISBN Unavailable. $5. Gr. 5-9.
    This is the fantastic story of three Yámana Indian boys
and one girl who were left on board a British vessel in
1826. One of them died shortly afterwards. The others
were taken to England, dressed like Europeans, and presented to the King and Queen of England. Although some
people treated them as savages, the King and Queen were
impressed by their politeness and gave Fueguia, the girl,
a wedding trousseau. A few years later they returned to
Argentina. One of the boys, York Minster, and Fueguia
fell in love and were married; the other, Jimmy Button,
became the controversial leader of the Yámana Indians.
Some believed he killed many of his former English friends;
others believed he simply remained confused as to which
was a better life--the English or his tribe.
    This is a well-told legend, with bold black-and-white
illustrations, which will impress readers with its depiction
of life in the southernmost tip of Argentina in the early
1800's.

Ipuana, Ramón Paz. El conejo y el mapurite [The Rabbit and
the Skunk]. Adapted by Verónica Uribe. Illustrated by
Vicky Sempere. Caracas: Ediciones Ekaré-Banco del
Libro, 1979. 36p. ISBN Unavailable. $4. Gr. 2-4.
    This is a traditional tale from the Guajiro peninsula in

Venezuela. It tells about a skunk who is also a witch doctor and who is on his way to cure a sick patient. On the road he meets a rabbit who deceives him three times. When the skunk realizes what the rabbit is up to, he decides to outsmart the rabbit. Alluring color and black-and-white illustrations complement the tale. (See also Paz Ipuana.)

Jiménez-Landi Martínez, Antonio. Leyendas de España [Spanish Legends]. Illustrated by Ricardo Zamorano. Madrid: Aguilar, 1977. 80p. ISBN 84-03-450-88-5. $9. Gr. 5-10.
This is a splendid collection of nine Spanish legends of the Middle Ages and the Renaissance period with handsome illustrations. The legends represent diverse Spanish geographic regions, such as Castile, Asturias, Galicia, and others.

Jones, Harold. Fábulas de Esopo [Tales from Aesop]. Illustrated by the author. Translated by José Emilio Pacheco. México: Promexa, 1982. 40p. ISBN 968-34-0179-1. $5. Gr. 4-8.
For full entry see series title, Clásicos infantiles ilustrados Promexa, in Section III.

Jordana Laguna, José Luis. Leyendas amazónicas [Legends of the Amazon]. Madrid: Doncel, 1976. 138p. ISBN 84-325-0560-9. $13. Gr. 3-10.
Excellent collection of 21 Peruvian legends of the Amazon region written in a most delightful, natural style. In brief, spontaneous narratives, the authors explain why it rains on the earth, the origin of the sun and the moon, children's proper behavior, why the sun shines every day, bird's happiness, the early cooking habits of humans, the origin of the Amazon River, and many other important aspects of life in the Amazon jungle. Colorful illustrations complement each legend.

Kurtycz, Marcos, and Ana García Kobeh. De tigres y tlacuaches: leyendas animales [Of Tigers and Panthers: Animal Legends]. México: Organización Editorial Novaro, 1981. 46p. ISBN 96-848-0001-0. $5. Gr. 5-9.
This excellent adaptation of six Mexican legends about

animals will charm readers with their wit and resourceful-
ness. It includes legends about the marriage of a humming-
bird, the shrewdness of a tiger, the punishment of a bat,
the dream of a fly, the stubbornness of a turtle, and the
mistake of a dog. Striking animal illustrations complement
each legend.

LaFontaine, Jean de. La tortuga y los dos patos [The Turtle
and the Two Ducks]. Illustrated by Anne Rockwell. Translated by Ana Luz Trejo. México: Promexa, 1982. 40p.
ISBN 968-34-0181-3. $5. Gr. 4-8.
For full entry see series title, Clásicos infantiles ilustrados Promexa, in Section III.

Lang, Andrew. Aladino y la lámpara maravillosa [Aladdin and
the Wonderful Lamp]. Illustrated by Errol Le Cain. Translated by José Emilio Pacheco. México: Promexa, 1982.
40p. ISBN 968-34-0182-1. $5. Gr. 4-8.
For full entry see series title, Clásicos infantiles ilustrados Promexa, in Section III.

Leal de Noguera, María. Cuentos viejos [Old Tales]. Illustrated by Osvaldo Salas. San José: Editorial Costa Rica,
1981. 171p. ISBN Unavailable. $6. Gr. 6-8.
This is the fifth edition of this well-known collection
of 24 traditional tales from Costa Rica, originally published
in 1938. In a marvelous, simple style, Mrs. Noguera relates the adventures of Uncle Rabbit as he outsmarts Uncle
Tiger, as well as the undertakings of courageous princes
and kind princesses and many others. Unfortunately, the
two-tone, trite illustrations do not do justice to the excitement of these tales.
Young children will also enjoy listening to these tales in
spite of the homely presentation of this collection.

Lyra, Carmen. Cuentos de mi tía Panchita [My Aunt Pan-
chita's Stories]. Illustrated by Juan Manuel Sanchez. San
José: Editorial Costa Rica, 1984. 190p. ISBN 9977-23-
135-4. $6. Gr. 6-10.
Outstanding collection that includes 23 tales from Costa
Rica. In a gracious, fast-moving style, the author relates

the tales as she heard them from her Aunt Panchita. They
tell about the devil's mother-in-law, a fool who wasn't stu-
pid, beautiful maidens, and courageous young men, as
well as ten stories about Uncle Rabbit outsmarting his
friends and enemies. The bland, monotone, line illustrations and the simple presentation of this publication hide
the wonderful enjoyment that these tales can provide to
young readers. These tales also can be read aloud to
young children who will undoubtedly enjoy their inherent
wit and excitement.

El maravilloso mundo de las fábulas [The Marvelous World of
Fables]. Valencia: Editorial Alfredo Ortells, 1984. 30p.
ISBN 84-7189-198-0. $12. Gr. 5-9.
    Fourteen well-known fables of the Spanish-speaking
world are included in this attractive publication with large
colorful illustrations. A simple moral at the end of each
fable summarizes the fable's intent. The fast pace and
excitement of these fables make them also appropriate for
reading aloud to younger children.

Mayer, Marianna. La bella y la bestia [Beauty and the Beast].
Illustrated by Mercer Mayer. Spanish version: José
Emilio Pacheco. México: Promociones Editoriales Mexicanas, 1982. [48p.] ISBN 968-34-0167-8. $5. Gr. 5-8.
    Good translation of Beauty and the Beast with outstand-
ing illustrations.

El morrocoy y el llanero [The Turtle and the Plainsman]. Illustrated by Carlos A. Chapman I. Caracas: R. J. Ediciones, 1984? [12p.] ISBN Unavailable. $3.50. Gr. 2-
4.
    A "morrocoy," a turtle that abounds in Venezuela, and
a plainsman were comparing the relative advantages of
their lives. The plainsman felt sorry for the heavy load
that the turtle carried on its back. Suddenly, the plainsman was stung by a bee and the turtle reminded him, as
it proceeded its slow march, that a small inconvenience is
all right if it provides some benefits. Lively, colorful illustrations complement the text.

Movischoff Zavala, Paulina. El cóndor de la vertiente: leyenda salasaca [The Condor of the Spring: Salasacan Legend]. Illustrated by Oswaldo Viteri. Quito: Ediciones del Sol Cia Ltda, 1978. [24p.] ISBN Unavailable. $3. Gr. 4-10.

This beautiful pre-Columbian legend from Ecuador tells how a condor (a large South American vulture) loved and protected the Salasaca people. He lived alone in a huge cavern, but one day he became lonely and took Mallu Quinche, the prettiest Salasaca maiden, to live with him. She was very unhappy, and her parents had given up all hope of ever seeing her again. Suddenly, Mallu Quinche returned home and gave birth to a feathered being--half man and half bird--and died shortly thereafter. Since then, no unmarried woman goes to the water spring, and the condor is again alone and sad.

Distinctive colorful illustrations add much excitement to this legend. (Some readers might object to a scene in which Mallu Quinche is shown bathing nude in the miraculous spring. It is done in such good taste, however, that only prudish adults will have any cause to object.)

Papp Severo, Emöke de. El bondadoso hermano menor [The Kindly Younger Brother]. Illustrated by Diane Goode. Translated by Felipe Garrido. México: Promexa, 1982. 40p. ISBN 968-34-0174-0. $5. Gr. 4-8.

For complete entry see series title, Clásicos infantiles ilustrados Promexa, in Section III.

Paz Ipuana, Ramón. El burrito y la tuna [The Small Burro and The Prickly Pear]. Adapted by Kukurusa. Illustrated by Amelie Areco. Caracas: Ediciones Ekaré, 1983. 35p. ISBN Unavailable. $4.50. Gr. 2-4.

Traditional folktale from Venezuela that tells how a brave donkey became a prickly pear with sweet fruit, and his conceited master became a prickly pear with bitter fruit. Soft pastel illustrations beautifully depict the desert scenes where this tale originated. (See also Ipuana, Ramón Paz.)

Perrault, Charles. La cenicienta o el zapatito de cristal [Cinderella or the Little Glass Slipper]. Illustrated by Errol Le Cain. Translated by José Emilio Pacheco. México: Promexa, 1982. 40p. ISBN 968-34-0184-8. $5. Gr. 4-8.

For full entry see series title, Clásicos infantiles ilustrados Promexa, in Section III.

Perrault, Charles. Pulgarcito y otros cuentos [Tom Thumb
and Other Stories]. Translated by Carmen Bravo-Villasante.
Illustrated by Klaus Encikat. Madrid: Editorial Doncel,
1983. 105p. ISBN 84-325-0389-4. $14. Gr. 6-Adult.
This excellent translation of Perrault's original stories
will delight readers of all ages. It includes "Tom Thumb,"
"Little Red Riding Hood," "Cinderella," "Puss in Boots,"
"Riquet with the Quiff," "The Fairies," "Blue Beard,"
"Donkey Skin," and " Sleeping Beauty."
The translator made a serious attempt to remain as close
as possible to the original edition published in 1697. Thus,
she maintained the simplicity and excitement of the stories
as well as the violence, gory scenes, and morals that Perrault appended at the end of each story. Each story includes two or three gorgeous full-page illustrations in color.

Pushkin, Alexander. El cuento del gallo de oro [The Tale of
the Golden Rooster]. Illustrated by I. Bilibin. Translated
by José Emilio Pacheco. Mexico, Promexa, 1982. 40p.
ISBN 968-34-0175-9. $5. Gr. 4-8.
For full entry see series title, Clásicos infantiles ilustrados Promexa, in Section III.

Pushkin, Alexander. El cuento del zar Saltán o el príncipe
y la princesa-cisne [The Tale of the Czar Saltán on the
Swan-Prince and Swan-Princess]. Illustrated by I. Bilibin.
Translated by José Emilio Pacheco. Mexico: Promexa,
1982. 40p. ISBN 968-34-0169-4. $5. Gr. 4-8.
For full entry see series title, Clásicos infantiles ilustrados Promexa, in Section III.

Rivero Oramas, Rafael. La piedra del Zamuro [Zamuro's
Stone]. Illustrated by Susana López. Caracas: Ediciones
Ekaré-Banco del Libro, 1981. [24p.] ISBN Unavailable.
$3. Gr. 3-6.
Uncle Rabbit is sad because he cannot fight with fero-
cious animals. Uncle Morrocoy (the turtle) tells him that
the best protection against danger is the little white stone

that is guarded by King Zamuro. Thus, Uncle Rabbit decides to obtain the magic stone. This traditional tale from Venezuela is exquisitely written and simply illustrated.

Ross, Tony. El frijol mágico [The Magic Bean]. Spanish version: José Emilio Pacheco. México: Promociones Editoriales Mexicanas, 1982. 26p. ISBN 968-34-0165-1. $3. Gr. 3-5.
   Good translation of Jack and the Beanstalk with charming illustrations.

Schkolnik, Saul. Cuentos del Tío Juan, el zorro culpeo [Uncle John's Stories. The Dark-Colored Fox]. Santiago: Empresa Editora Zig-Zag, S.A., 1982. 87p. ISBN Unavailable. $7. Gr. 4-7.
   Eleven amusing folktales from Chile about Uncle Juan, the fox, and his numerous friends--the animals that inhabit Northern Chile--are included in this simple collection. In addition to the spontaneous adventures of Uncle Juan as he tries to outsmart his friends, the author has included brief descriptive notes and sketches about each animal discussed in the tales. It is unfortunate that the poor presentation of this publication--cheap paper and homely black-and-white illustrations--actually might discourage young readers.

El tigre y el rabipelado [The Tiger and the Porcupine]. Illustrated by Carlos A. Chapman I. Caracas: R. J. Ediciones, 1984? [12p.] ISBN Unavailable. $3.50. Gr. 2-4.
   Tiger's dream was to catch porcupine. Thus, when porcupine was about to drown, tiger saved him with the understanding that tiger could eat him as soon as he dried up. But again, porcupine ran away from tiger's claws. Colorful illustrations complement the easy-to-read text.

Uslar Pietri, Arturo. El conuco de tío conejo [Uncle Rabbit's Maize Field]. Illustrated by Jorge Blanco. Caracas: Ediciones María Di Mase, 1984. [22p.] ISBN Unavailable. $2.50. Gr. 6-9.
   This delightful Venezuelan tale, originally published in

Argentina in 1949, tells about Uncle Rabbit's use of deceit
and trickery to outsmart the abuses of the powerful and
strong Uncle Tiger. This lighthearted tale is an excellent
introduction to the distinguished Venezuelan author Arturo
Uslar Pietri, despite its modest presentation--simple black-
and-white illustrations, and unattractive pamphlet-style
format.

Vallverdú, Josep. La perla negra [The Black Pearl]. Illustrated by Horacio Elena. Barcelona: La Galera, S.A.,
1982. 54p. ISBN 84-246-3810-7. $5. Gr. 4-7.
    This fast-paced story is based on an old legend. It
tells how a magic substance--a black pearl--can change the
life of its owner. Sabir, a poor but honest fisherman,
barely made a living from the sea. When he found the
black pearl, he asked for immense riches and power and
forgot about all the poor people. His third wish made him
see his own greed and ask for forgiveness. Simple two-
tone illustrations complement the text.

Yalí. Las trampas del Curupí y otras leyendas [Curupí's
Traps and Other Legends]. Buenos Aires: Central
Editor de America Latina, 1976. 30p. ISBN Unavailable.
$5. Gr. 5-8.
    Two lively legends from Argentina are included. "Las
trampas del Curupí" tells why Indian mothers in Argentina
are calm and allow their children to play far away from
home only while the "Curupí" sleeps. "Eireté la indiecita"
tells how Eireté, a lovely Indian girl, learned how to
weave the beautiful "ñanduti" fabric. It is indeed unfortunate that the illustrations do not do justice to these
tales; they are blurred patches of color which lack imagina-
tion.

462 SPANISH ETYMOLOGY

Cervera, Juan. La leyenda de la palabras [Legend of Words].
Illustrated by Felipe López Salam. Valladolid: Editorial
Miñón, 1983. 101p. ISBN 84-355-0671-1. $7. Gr. 6-12.
    The history and meaning of 132 Spanish words are told
in an amusing and engaging manner. It contains explanations of well-known words, such as "nicotina" (nicotine),

"corbata" (necktie), "cursi" (vulgar), "tiovivo" (merry-
go-round), "azafata" (stewardess), and many others.
Colorful illustrations add interest to the simply-written explanations.

463 DICTIONARIES AND LEXICOGRAPHY

McNaught, Harry. 500 palabras nuevas para ti/500 Words to
Grow On. Translated by Pilar de Cuenca and Inés Alvarez. New York: Random House, 1982. 32p. ISBN 0-
39-4851455. $1.95. Gr. 1-5.
Names of various objects in Spanish and English with
accompanying illustrations are grouped in topics such as
colors, people, clothing, toys, kitchen, food, vehicles, the
country, and others. The clear illustrations and the selection of objects well known to children make this book a
good introduction to the study of a second language. The
original English version was published in 1973.

465 SPANISH STRUCTURAL SYSTEM (GRAMMAR)

Greenfield, Eric V. Spanish Grammar. New York: Barnes
and Noble Books, 1971. 236p. ISBN 0-06-460042. $5.50.
Gr. 6-Adult.
This book includes the essentials of Spanish grammar for
those beginning the study of the language. It identifies,
explains, and exemplifies the high points of Spanish grammar through readings and translation exercises.

Terrell, Tracy D., and Maruxa Salgues de Cargill. Lingüista
aplicada a la enseñanza del español a anglohablantes [Ap-
plied Linguistics to the Teaching of Spanish to English
Speakers]. New York: John Wiley and Sons, 1979. 218p.
ISBN 0-471-03946-2. $23. Gr. 8-Adult.
Serious English-speaking students of the Spanish language may find this guide to Spanish grammar and phonol-
ogy practical. It is definitely not for children.

500 PURE SCIENCES INCLUDING NATURAL SCIENCES

Kincaid, Lucy. Mira abajo [Look Down]. ISBN 84-241-5314-6.

_____. Mira adentro [Look Inside]. ISBN 84-241-5316-2.

_____. Mira alrededor [Look Around]. ISBN 84-241-5315-4.

_____. Mira arriba [Look Up]. ISBN 84-241-5313-8.

Ea. vol.: [20p.] Illustrated by Eric Kincaid. Translated by A. Larrosa. Colección las gafas mágicas. León:
Spain Editorial Everest, 1982. $3. Gr. 3-6.

By superposing a realistic illustration over an allegor-
ical one, these books encourage children to observe nature. Each page is devoted to an animal or concept and
includes the correct Spanish word and a brief sentence explaining a special characteristic of the animal or concept.
Mira abajo tells about frogs, snakes, lizards, dragonflies,
small fish, snails. Mira adentro tells about rabbits, bub-
bles, nests, nuts, seeds, oranges. Mira alrededor tells
about butterflies, bees, spiders, ants, worms. Mira arriba
tells about birds, flying insects, drops of water, snow
flakes, the moon, stars, clouds. Even though these books
do not include an index or a table of contents, they are
indeed a delightful introduction to nature.

502.8 PURE SCIENCES, TECHNIQUES, PROCEDURES,
              APPARATUS, MATERIALS

Peñarroja, Jordi. Juega con ... el aire [Play with ... Air].
ISBN 84-02-06884-7.

Peñarroja, Jordi, and Josep M. Bonet. Juega con ... el
agua 2 [Play with ... Water]. ISBN 84-02-06900-2.

_____. Juega con ... el calor 3 [Play with ... Heat].
ISBN 84-02-06901-0.

_____. Juega con ... la luz 4 [Play with ... Light].
ISBN 84-02-06902-9.

_____. Juega con ... la electricidad y el magnetismo 5
[Play with ... Electricity and Magnetism]. ISBN 84-02-
-6903-7.

_____. Juega con ... la química 6 [Play with ... Chem-
istry]. ISBN 84-02-06904-5.

Ea. vol.: 48p. Color photographs. Barcelona: Editorial Bruguera, 1981. $5.50. Gr. 6-8.
This series encourages young readers to have fun by making simple experiments with things that are readily available in most homes. The concepts of air, water, heat, light, electricity, and chemistry are made familiar to children through these easy-to-make experiments. Clear, color photographs describe each experiment.

507.2 RESEARCH TECHNIQUES IN SCIENCE

Cobb, Vicki. Experimentos científicos que se pueden comer [Scientific Experiments That Can Be Eaten]. Illustrated by Peter Lippman. New York: J. B. Lippincott, 1979. 141p. ISBN 0-397-31887-I. $9.89. Gr. 5-9.
By using the kitchen and common kitchen utensils, the author explains how young readers can make 39 experiments with food which demonstrate various scientific principles with edible results. It includes fruit drinks, salad dressings, mayonnaise, jellies, muffins, chop suey, yogurt, vegetables, and others.

508 DESCRIPTIONS AND SURVEYS OF NATURAL PHENOMENA

Wicks, Keith. Ciencia recreativa [Science Can Be Fun]. Barcelona: Marcombo Boixaneu Editores, 1984. 32p. (Biblioteca Técnica Juvenil). ISBN 84-267-0538-3. $8.95. Gr. 6-10.
For full annotation see series title in Section III.

520 ASTRONOMY AND ALLIED SCIENCES

Osman, Tony. El descubrimiento del universo [Discovery of the Universe]. Madrid: Ediciones Plesa, 1977. 48p. ISBN 84-7374-048-3. $6. Gr. 6-10.
For full entry see series title, El Museo de los Descubrimientos, in Section III.

Pérez de Laborda, Alfonso. Los antiguos astrónomos [The Ancient Astronomers]. Adapted by Raffaele Fatone. Il-

lustrated by Sandro Corsi. (El Hombre y el Cosmos).
Madrid: Ediciones Encuentro, 1984. [44p.] ISBN 84-
7490-099-0. $9.50. Gr. 6-9.
   In 20 brief chapters with excellent colorful illustrations,
young readers are introducted to the world's greatest astronomers and their fascinations with the structure, origin,
and beauty of the universe. It tells about prehistoric man,
Egyptians, Jews, ancient Greeks, Chinese, Hindus, Mayas,
the Arabs, Copernicus, Kepler, Galileo and Newton's con-
tributions to modern astronomy. There is a minor flaw in
this otherwise good overview to ancient astronomers: The
people who perform religious rites in a Jewish temple are
mistakenly referred to as priests, rather than rabbis.
Other titles in this series are La astronomía moderna [Mod-
ern Astronomy] and La formación del universo [The Forma-
tion of the Universe].

Von Schweinitz, Dagmar. El niño pregunta: el tiempo, el
sol, la luna y las estrellas [A Child Asks: Time, Sun,
Moon, and Stars]. Translated by Mariano y Rafael Orta.
Barcelona: Ediciones Toray, 1981. 59p. ISBN 84-310-
2334-1. $9. Gr. 6-9.
   Simple explanation and excellent color photographs describe basic facts about the weather, the sun, the moon,
and the stars. It includes answers to such simple questions as, Where do the clouds go? What is fog? How high
is the sky? Do the stars move?

523 DESCRIPTIVE ASTRONOMY

Dultzin, Deborah, and others. De la tierra al cosmos: astronomía para niños [From the Earth to the Cosmos: Astronomy for Children]. Illustrated by Diego Echegaray
and Juan González de León. México: Cidcli, 1984. 50p.
$6.95. Gr. 6-9.
   For full entry see series title, La Brújula, in Section
III.

Lewellen, John. La luna, el sol, y las estrellas [Moon, Sun
and Stars]. Translated by Lada Kratky. Photographs,
drawings, index. (Asi es mi mundo). Chicago: Children's
Press, 1984. 48p. ISBN 0-516-31637-0. $8.95. Gr. 2-4.
   For full annotation see series title in Section III.

523.2 SOLAR SYSTEM

Spamer, Irene. El universo [The Universe]. Illustrated by
María Figueroa. Mexico: Editorial Patria, 1981. 42p.
ISBN 968-39-0003-8. $5. Gr. 2-4.
   In a brief and simple style, two children describe their
experiences as they travel in the universe: They visit
the moon and a spaceship, and they come close to the sun.
One of the children also imagines Saturn. Appropriate il-
lustrations complement the text.

523.3 MOON

Usborne, Peter, and Su Swallow. La luna [Moon]. Barcelona:
Editorial Molino, 1981. 24p. ISBN 84-272-5007-X. $3.
Gr. 1-3.
   For full entry see series title, Biblioteca Educativa In-
fantil Molino, in Section III.

523.7 SUN

Usborne, Peter, and Su Swallow. El sol [Sun]. Barcelona:
Editorial Molino, 1981. 24p. ISBN 84-272-5011-8. $3.
Gr. 1-3.
   For full entry see series title, Biblioteca Educativa In-
fantil Molino, in Section III.

525 EARTH (ASTRONOMICAL GEOGRAPHY)

Grée, Alain. Tom e Irene descubren las estaciones [Tom and
Irene Discover the Seasons]. Illustrated by Gerard Grée.
Barcelona: Editorial Juventud, 1979. 21p. (Serie Tom
e Irene). ISBN 84-261-5593-6. $3.50. Gr. 4-6.
   Young readers are exposed to the change of seasons
through Tom and Irene's observations of nature. They notice
the sun, flowers, and animals during the different seasons
and comment on the weather, activities, and clothing required for each season. Attractive illustrations complement the informative text.

Provensen, Alice, and Martin Provensen. El libro de las es-

taciones/A Book of Seasons. Translated by Pilar de Cuenca
and Inés Alvarez. New York: Random House, 1982. 32p.
ISBN 0-394-95143-3. $4.99. Gr. K-2.
 These are easy-to-read bilingual descriptions of the
changing seasons with appropriate illustrations of activities
that children can readily understand. Simple Spanish sentences are followed by English sentences on the same page.

529 TIME (CHRONOLOGY)

Solano Flores, Guillermo. La noche [The Night]. Illustrated
by Silvia Luz Alvarado. México: Editorial Trillas, 1986.
16p. ISBN 968-24-1781-3. $3. Gr. 2-4.
 Tells about nighttime activities. For full entry see
series title, Ojos abiertos, in Section III.

530 PHYSICS

La física [Physics]. Barcelona: Afha Internacional, 1979.
52p. ISBN Unavailable. $6. Gr. 5-8.
 For full entry see series title, El hombre y su entorno,
in Section III.

535.6 COLOR

Usborne, Peter, and Su Swallow. Color [Color]. Barcelona:
Editorial Molino, 1981. 24p. ISBN 84-272-5014-2. $3.
Gr. 1-3.
 For full entry see series title, Biblioteca educativa
infantil Molino, in Section III.

549 MINERALOGY

Los minerales [Minerals]. Barcelona: Afha Internacional,
1979. 52p. ISBN Unavailable. $6. Gr. 5-8.
 For full entry see series title, El hombre y su entorno,
in Section III.

551 GEOLOGY, METEOROLOGY, HYDROLOGY

Lambert, David. Actividad de la tierra [Earth's Activities].

Madrid: Editorial Everest, 1982. 41p. Color photos and
drawings. ISBN 84-241-5706-0. $5. Gr. 6-9.
For full entry see series title, Colección Orbita, in Section III.

551.4 GEOMORPHOLOGY AND GENERAL HYDROLOGY

Denou, Violeta. El Mar [The Sea]. Barcelona: Ediciones
Hymsa, 1980. 26p. Illustrated by the authors. ISBN 84-
7183-164-3. $3. Gr. 4-7.
For full entry see series title, El hombre y la naturaleza,
in Section III.

Gr&e, Alain. El agua [Water]. Barcelona: Editorial Juventud,
1981. 29p. ISBN 84-261-1706-6. $3. Gr. 4-6.
For full entry see series title, Serie Germán y Ana, in
Section III.

Mayoral, María Teresa. El libro del agua y la vida [Book of
Water and Life]. Illustrated by Matías Rivera. León:
Editorial Nebrija, 1980. 69p. ISBN 84-391-2009-5. $7.50.
Gr. 6-9.
For full entry see series title, El Libro de ..., in Sec-
tion III.

Von Schweinitz, Dagmar. El niño pregunta: el mar, las
montañas [A Child Asks: The Sea and the Mountains].
Translated by Mariano y Rafael Orta. Barcelona: Ediciones Toray, 1981. 57p. ISBN 84-310, 2391-0. $9. Gr.
6-9.
Simple explanations and excellent color photographs describe basic facts about the sea and about mountains. It
includes answers to such simple questions as, Why is sea
water salty? Do sharks eat only men? Why are there
waves? How were mountains born? Why are there so many
streams in the mountains?

551.5 METEOROLOGY
(including mechanics of atmosphere)

Denou, Violeta. La fuerza de la naturaleza [Nature's Force].

Barcelona: Ediciones Hymsa, 1980. 26p. Illustrated by
the author. ISBN 84-7183-133-3. $3. Gr. 4-7.
For full entry see series title, El hombre y la naturaleza, in Section III.

Solano Flores, Guillermo. El viento [The Wind]. Illustrated
by Norma Josefina and Patina Dominguez. México: Editorial Trillas, 1986. 16p. ISBN 968-24-1817-2. $3. Gr.
2-4.
Describes what happens when there is a lot of wind.
For full entry see series title, Ojos abiertos, in Section
III.

551.57 HYDROMETEOROLOGY
(including rain and snow)

Solano Flores, Guillermo. La lluvia [The Rain]. Illustrated
by Silvia Luz Alvarado. México: Editorial Trillas, 1986.
16p. ISBN 968-24-1778-3. $3. Gr. 2-4.
Shows what happens when it rains. For full entry see
series title, Ojos abiertos, in Section III.

Usborne, Peter, and Su Swallow. Lluvia [Rain]. Barcelona:
Editorial Molino, 1981. 24p. ISBN 84-272-5001-0. $3.
Gr. 1-3.
For full entry see series title, Biblioteca Educativa In-
fantil Molino, in Section III.

Usborne, Peter, and Su Swallow. Nieve [Snow]. Barcelona:
Editorial Molino, 1981. 24p. ISBN 84-272-5012-6. $3.
Gr. 1-3.
For full entry see series title, Biblioteca Educativa In-
fantil Molino, in Section III.

551.6 CLIMATOLOGY AND WEATHER

Ford, Adam. Observando el clima [Observing the Climate].
Madrid: Editorial Everest, 1982. 41p. Color photos and
drawings. ISBN 84-241-5704-4. $5. Gr. 6-9.
For full entry see series title, Colección Orbita, in Section III.

553 ECONOMIC GEOLOGY

Denou, Violeta. La tierra y sus riquesas [The Earth's Riches].
Barcelona: Ediciones Hymsa, 1980. Illustrated by the author. ISBN Unavailable. $3. Gr. 4-7.
For full entry see series title, El hombre y la naturaleza,
in Section III.

560 PALEONTOLOGY, PALEOZOOLOGY

Los animales prehistóricos [Prehistoric animals]. Barcelona:
Afha Internacional, 1979. 52p. ISBN Unavailable. $6.
Gr. 5-8.
For complete entry see the series title, El hombre y su
entorno, in Section III.

567.9 FOSSIL REPTILES, INCLUDING DINOSAURS

Clark, Mary Lou. Dinosaurios [Dinosaurs]. Translated by
Lada Kratky. (Asi es mi mundo.) Chicago: Childrens
Press, 1984. 48p. ISBN 0-516-31612-5). Photographs,
drawings, index. $8.95. Gr. 2-4.
For annotation see series title in Section III.

574 BIOLOGY

Dos cuentos de vida [Two Life Stories]. Illustrated by Carlos
A. Chapman I. Caracas: R. J. Ediciones, 1984. 12p.
ISBN Unavailable. $4. Gr. 2-4.
The life cycles of a plant and a bird are described in
a simple text and amusing illustrations in color.

574.1 BIOLOGY, PHYSIOLOGY

Schkolnick, Saul. Colorín colorado, ovulito fecundado [End
of Story, ... Fertilized Ovum]. Santiago de Chile: Editorial Universitaria, 1981. 59p. ISBN Unavailable. $7.
Gr. 5-8.
In an amusing manner, the author explains the most
common forms of reproduction: "Colorín colorado" shows
in a witty and light manner the union of sperm and an

ovum; "Tú para allullá" shows the process of meiosis: "Pequeño intermedio" tells about pollination; "Operación semilla" shows the fertilization of a plant; and "Huevos cascarudos" tells about the change in the evolution of species from soft eggs to protected eggs. Bright, delightful illustrations complement this witty introduction to the process of life itself.

574.5 ECOLOGY

Cárdenas, Magolo. La zona del silencio [The Silent Zone]. Illustrated by the author. México: Editorial Patria, 1984. 31p. ISBN 968-39-0077-1. $3. Gr. 1-3.
    For full entry see series title, Colección Piñata, in Section III.

Catchpole, Clive. Desiertos [Deserts]. Illustrated by Brian McIntyre. ISBN 84-7527-208-7.

_____. Junglas [Jungles]. Illustrated by Denise Finney. ISBN 84-7525-207-9.

_____. Montañas [Mountains]. Illustrated by Brian McIntyre. ISBN 84-7525-206-0.

_____. Praderas [Grasslands]. Illustrated by Peter Snowball. ISBN 84-7525-205-2.

    Ea. vol.: [26p.] (Mundo Vivo). Madrid: Ediciones Generales Anaya, 1985. $7.95. Gr. 5-9.
    Deserts, jungles, mountains, and grasslands are introduced to young readers through a straightforward text and excellent illustrations in color. Each volume explains how plants and animals depend upon each other and how they adapt to their particular habitat.

Giron, Nicole. El mar [The Sea]. Illustrated by Leonel Maciel. México: Editorial Patria, 1981. 44p. ISBN 96-839-0000-3. $5. Gr. 3-5.
    Life by the sea is simply described in this easy-to-read book. It tells about the vastness of the ocean, the beauty of marine life, the excitement of fishing, and other activities.

The modernistic water-color illustrations add animation to
the story, even though they are too vague to be informative.

Sabugo Pintor, Angel. El libro del medio ambiente [Book of
the Environment]. Illustrated by Constantino Gatagan.
León: Editorial Nebrija, 1980. 76p. ISBN 84-391-2005-2.
$7.50. Gr. 6-9.
For full entry see series title, El libro de ..., in Section III.

581 GENERAL BOTANY

Neigoff, Anne. Los lugares donde viven las plantas [Where
Plants Live].

_____. Muchas plants [Many Plants].

_____. Las plantas que necesitamos [Plants We Need].

_____. Las plantas y como crecen [How Plants Grow].

_____. Las plantas y sus semillas [Plants and Their Seeds].

Ea. vol.: 32p. Illustrated by James G. Teason. Translated by Robbe Lynn Henderson and others. (Ahora Cono-
ces). Chicago: Encyclopaedia Britannica Education Corporation, 1973. ISBN 0-87827-171-6. $99. Gr. 4-6.
Well-done Spanish translation of the series "Now You
Know About Plants," which offers children many opportunities to observe and compare sizes, shapes, textures, and
the changing cycles of plant growth. A teacher's guide
written in English suggests other learning activities. Los
lugares donde viven las plantas explores the many places
where plants live. Muchas plantas introduces children to
the variety of plant life and to the common properties plants
share as living things. Las plantas que necesitamos explains the many ways we use plants in our daily lives.
Las plantas y como crecen explains the functions of plant
parts and the varied ways plants grow. Las plantas y sus
semillas tells about the variety of ways seeds differ in size,
shape, color, and dispersal. Each book has a correlated
cassette.

Pavord, Anna. Botánica recreativa [Growing Things]. Barcelona: Marcombo Boixareu Editores, 1984. 32p. (Biblioteca Técnica Juvenil). ISBN 84-267-0537-5. $8.95. Gr.
6-10.
For full annotation see series title in Section III.

582.16 TREES

Los árboles [Trees]. Barcelona: Afha Internacional, 1979.
52p. ISBN Unavailable. $6. Gr. 5-8.
For full entry see series title, El hombre y su entorno,
in Section III.

Usborne, Peter, and Su Swallow. Arboles [Trees]. Barcelona:
Editorial Molino, 1981. 24p. ISBN 84-272-5018-5. $3. Gr.
1-3.
For full entry see series title, Biblioteca Educativa Infantil Molino, in Section III.

590.74 ZOOLOGY--MUSEUMS, COLLECTIONS, EXHIBITS
(including zoos)

Ferrán, Jaime. Mañana de parque [Morning at the Park].
Illustrated by Viví Escrivá. Salamanca: Anaya, 1972.
85p. ISBN 84-207-0885-2. $9. Gr. K-2.
Gorgeous illustrations of children visiting a zoo; 35
animals are described in humorous detail.

591 ZOOLOGY

Los animales de la casa y del jardín [House and Garden Ani-
mals].

Los animales del campo y de la granja [Country and Farm
Animals].

Los animales del bosque y del monte [Forest and Mountain
Animals].

Los animales del río y del estanque [River and Pond Animals].

Los animales del lago y del pantano [Lake and Dam Animals].

Los animales de la montaña y el valle [Valley and Mountain Animals].

Los animales de la tundra y de los hielos [Animals of the Tundra and Ice Region].

Los animales de la playa y de la costa [Beach and Coastal Animals].

Los animales del mar y de las lagunas [Lakes and Sea Animals].

Los animales del océano y de los abismos [Animals of Ocean].

Los animales de Africa [African Animals].

Los animales de América del Sur [South American Animals].

Los animales de Asia [Asian Animals].

Los animales de América del Norte [North American Animals].

Los animales de Oceanía [Ocean Animals].

Los animales de la prehistoria [Prehistoric Animals].

Los animales de la sabana africana [Animals of the African Savannah].

Los animales de la selva y estepa africana [Animals of the African Jungle and Plains].

Los animales de los ríos y los lagos de Africa [Animals of the African Rivers and Lakes].

Los animales de la pradera americana [Animals of the American Prairie].

Los animales de la selva amazónica [Animals of the Amazon Jungle].

Los animales de la jungla, estepas y montañas de Asia y Oceanía [Animals of the Jungles, Plains and Mountains of Asia and Oceania].

44 Basic Collection of Books in Spanish

Los animales de los llanos y montañas de Europa [Animals of the Valleys and Mountains of Europe].

Los animales marinos [Marine Animals].

Ea. vol.: 61p. (Vida Intima de los Animales). Barcelona: Afha Internacional, 1981. ISBN 84-201-0282-2 for the series. $5. Gr. 5-8.
Each book in this series describes the special characteristics and the environment in which various types of animals live. Attractive, colorful drawings are the main attraction, with one simple paragraph description about each animal. Unfortunately, there is no index. Readers should note that there are allusions to "God's creation of man" in providing a historical perspective. Notwithstanding these limitations, this is an excellent simple series about animals in their natural environments.

Jiménez-Landi Martínez, Antonio. El libro de los animales [The Animal Book]. Illustrated by F. Goico Aguirre. Spain: Aguilar, 1979. 56p. ISBN Unavailable. $7. Gr. 3-8.
Pleasing animal illustrations and one-paragraph descriptions tell about many animals' activities, customs, and lifestyles. It includes big and small animals from Europe, America, Asia, and Africa.

Manley, Deborah. Es divertido descubrir la vida de los animales [It Is Fun to Discover Animals' Lives]. Illustrated by Moira and Colin Maclean. Translated by José Ferrer Aleu. Barcelona: Plaza & Janés, Editores, 1981. 47p. ISBN 84-01-70098-1. $6. Gr. 4-7.
Basic facts about animals are explained through a simple text and illustrations. It tells about animals around the world, birds, penguins, monkeys, farm animals, dogs, cats, insects, reptiles, and others.

Zeff, Claudia. Los animales: un libro de palabras ilustrado [Animals: An Illustrated Word Book]. Illustrated by Nick Price. Barcelona: Plaza & Janes. S.A., 1983. 47p. ISBN 84-01-70171-6. $5. Gr. 2-4.
This picture wordbook about animals introduces young

children to many aspects of the animal kingdom through
amusing illustrations. A well-done index complements this
simple book.

591.03 ZOOLOGY. DICTIONARIES, ENCYCLOPEDIAS

Montes, Graciela. Gran enciclopedia de los pequeños [Chil-
drens' Great Encyclopedia]. Illustrated by Clara Urquijo
and others. Buenos Aires: Editorial La Encina, 1980.
[100p.] ISBN Unavailable. $9. Gr. 5-8.
  The title of this book is misleading; it is not an encyclopedia for young readers but a book with an interesting
manner of introducing animals to children. First, it includes a simple description that highlights important aspects of the animals' lives; then, it includes a traditional
Argentine legend where the specific animal is the main
character; last, it contains two pages of technical/scien-
tific information about each animal. The animals described in this book are "hornero," a common bird of Argentina; a fox, a cricket; an armadillo; an anteater; and
a toad.
  Animal lovers will be delighted with these engaging
stories and legends as well as with the amusing illustrations of animals in various situations.

595.78 LEPIDOPTERA

Ortiz Monasterio P., Fernando, and Valentina Ortiz Monasterio
Garza. Mariposa monarca vuelo de papel [Monarch butter-
fly: Paper Flight]. México: Cidcli, 1984. 62p. ISBN
968-494-009-2. $6.95. Gr. 6-9.
  For full entry see series title, Las Brújula, in Section
III.

597 COLD-BLOODED VERTEBRATES

Van Dulm, Sacha, and Jan Riem. Como vive un pez de río:
la vida de un espino [How a River Fish Lives: The Life
of a Stickleback]. Translated by María Puncel. Madrid:
Ediciones Altea, 1980. [30p.] ISBN 84-372-1466-1. $5.
Gr. 5-8.
  Attractive illustrations and a well-written text describe

the life cycle of a stickleback, a spiny river fish. It tells
about its eating and mating habits as well as the environment in which it lives.

597.98 CROCODILES AND ALLIGATORS

García Sánchez, José Luis, and Miguel Angel Pacheco. El
cocodrilo [The Crocodile]. Illustrated by Nella Bosnia.
Madrid: Ediciones Altea, 1979. 21p. ISBN 84-7348-009-0.
$3. Gr. K-3.
   Amusing illustrations and a simple text tell about the
life and special characteristics of a crocodile. Young readers will be delighted with the witty situations in which the
crocodile is shown brushing its 65 teeth, selecting its food
at the grocery store, and confronting a store salesman
with a display of crocodile products. It also contains basic
facts about crocodiles.

598 BIRDS

Las aves [Birds]. Barcelona: Afha Internacional, 1979. 52p.
   ISBN Unavailable. $6. Gr. 5-8.
   For full entry see series title, El hombre y su entorno,
in Section III.

Usborne, Peter, and Su Swallow. Aves [Birds]. Barcelona:
Editorial Molino, 1981. 24p. ISBN 84-272-5009-6. $3.
Gr. 1-3.
   For full entry see series title, Biblioteca Educativa In-
fantil Molino, in Section III.

599.4 ANSERIFORMES

Herring, Philippine, and Fetze Pijlman. Como vive un ave
acuática: el somormujo [How an Aquatic Bird Lives: The
Loon]. Translated by María Puncel. Madrid: Ediciones
Altea, 1981. [28p.] ISBN 84-372-1585-4. $3.50. Gr. 5-
8.
   Attractive illustrations and an informative text describe
the life of a loon, a fish-eating, diving bird. It tells about
its eating and mating habits as well as the environment in
which it lives.

599.73 MAMMALS, EVEN-TOED UNGULATES

García Sánchez, José Luis, and Miguel Angel Pacheco. La
jirafa [The Giraffe]. Illustrated by Nella Bosnia. Madrid:
Ediciones Altea, 1979. 18p. ISBN 84-372-1433-5. $3.
Gr. K-3.
  Humorous illustrations and a simple text tell about the
giraffe. Their height allows giraffes to discover enemies
from a great distance and to eat from the tallest trees.
Giraffes are also shown standing to go to sleep in a railroad car, going to a hospital to have a baby, and baby
giraffes running a few hours after birth.

599.74 MAMMALS, CARNIVORES

García Sánchez, José Luis, and Miguel Angel Pacheco. El
lobo [The Wolf]. Illustrated by Nella Bosnia. Madrid:
Ediciones Altea, 1980. 24p. ISBN 84-372-1416-5. $3.
Gr. K-3.
  Charming illustrations and a simple text tell about the
life and special characteristics of a wolf. Young readers
will enjoy the witty situations in which a wolf is shown:
going out at night to the opera after he rests during the
day, getting together with his friends in winter to go
hunting, running ahead of a group of athletes, and learning to play chess. It also contains basic facts about
wolves.

García Sánchez, José Luis, and Miguel Angel Pacheco. El
tigre [The Tiger]. Illustrated by Nella Bosnia. Madrid:
Ediciones Altea, 1980. 24p. ISBN 84-372-1415-7. $3.
Gr. K-3.
  Delightful illustrations and a simple text tell about the
life and special characteristics of a tiger. Young readers
will enjoy the witty situations in which a tiger is shown:
eating steak at a fancy restaurant, showing off its elegant
fur, and winning medals for being such a good swimmer.
It also contains basic facts about tigers.

Hogenweg, Martin, and Hans Dorrestijn. Como vive una
comadreja [The Life of a Weasel]. Madrid: Ediciones Altea,
1980. [30p.] ISBN 84-372-1467-X. $3.50. Gr. 5-8.

The life cycle of a weasel, a small carnivorous mammal, is described through attractive illustrations and a well-written text. It tells about its eating and mating habits as well as the environment in which it lives.

Planten, Annet, and Jan Riem. Como vive una nutria [How an Otter Lives]. Translated by María Puncel. Madrid: Ediciones Altea, 1981. [28p.] ISBN 84-372-1537-4. $4.50. Gr. 5-8.
Attractive illustrations and an informative text describe the life of an otter, an aquatic animal with dark brown fur. It tells about its eating and mating habits as well as the environment in which it lives.

604 GENERAL TECHNOLOGIES

Frontera: infinito hacia el 2000 con las nuevas tecnologías [Frontier: Infinite, Towards 2000 with the New Technologies]. (Colección Nuevas Fronteras). Buenos Aires: Editorial Sigmar, 1985. [94p.] ISBN 950-11-0393-5. $15.95. Gr. 6-12.
This book presents the most recent achievements of science and technology and proposes models of life in the new frontiers. The results are an exciting and well-written introduction to the world of computers, including artificial intelligence, personal computers, video games, robots, and other uses of computers. The last third of the book introduces the reader to genetic engineering, lasers, cultivated deserts, spaceships, and other marvels of technology. Excellent drawings and photographs in color as well as a brief dictionary of technical and scientific terms make this book a desirable introduction to modern technology.

608 INVENTIONS

Segrelles, Vicente. Historia ilustrada de los barcos [Illustrated History of Ships]. ISBN 84-201-0544-9.

_____. Historia ilustrada de la aviación desde los inicios hasta 1935 [Illustrated History of Aviation ... Beginning to 1935]. ISBN 84-201-0576-7.

_____, and Antonio Cunillera. Inventos que conmovieron al mundo [Inventions That Affected the World]. ISBN 84-201-0284-9.

_____, and _____. Descubrimientos e inventos [Discoveries and Inventions]. ISBN 84-201-0201-6.

Ea. vol.: 61p. (Enciclopedia Juvenil Auriga). Barcelona: Ediciones Afha, 1981. $7. Gr. 5-8.
These are four titles that deal with scientific and technical concepts from a series of seven volumes. The attractive presentation of each book--excellent colorful illustrations and brief, simple explanations--is sure to appeal to novices or confirmed readers. These are especially useful for arousing the interest of students in various inventions and discoveries, along with providing a historical overview of ships and airplanes up to 1935.

610.7306 NURSING ORGANIZATIONS AND PERSONNEL

Puncel, María. Cuando sea mayor seré enfermera [When I'm Older I Will Be a Nurse]. Illustrated by Ulises Wensell. Madrid: Ediciones Altea, 1980. 44p. ISBN 84-372-1390-8. $5. Gr. 5-8.
A young girl falls from her bicycle and is taken to the emergency ward at the hospital. There she learns about the importance of nurses in caring for sick people. Nurses are shown taking X-rays, assisting in surgery, feeding patients, making beds, analyzing blood, giving information, and many other activities. The informative text is complemented by interesting illustrations. Perhaps one should object to the sexual stereotypes: All the doctors in the story are males; all the nurses are females.

612 HUMAN PHYSIOLOGY

Boix, Federico. Padre, ¿cómo nace un niño? [Father, How Is a Child Born?] Barcelona: Editorial Nova Terra, 1971. 15p. ISBN 84-280-0476-5. $3. Gr. 3-6.
Straightforward approach, with excellent illustrations, to the birth of a child. Simple explanations are given by the father to a girl and boy upon the arrival of their new

50 Basic Collection of Books in Spanish

baby brother. Breast-feeding, birth, and affection are effectively explained.

El cuerpo humano [Human Body]. Barcelona: Afha Internacional, 1979. 52p. $6. Gr. 5-8.
For fuller entry see series title, El hombre y su entorno, in Section III.

Murphy, Chuck. Tu cuerpo [Your Body]. ISBN Unavailable.

_____. Tus sentidos [Your Senses]. ISBN Unavailable.

Ea. vol.: Illustrated by the author. Bogotá: Editorial Norma, 1982. [12p.] $7.50. Gr. 4-6.
Through simple explanations and clear illustrations in color, children are exposed to the physiology of the human body and the senses. Each book contains flaps, arrows, and pop-up figures that readers can move to depict realistically the various functions of the body and the senses. Tu cuerpo describes the skeletal, muscular, circulatory, respiratory, and digestive systems. Tus sentidos describes the eyes, ears, and the senses of smell, taste, and touch.

Rayner, Claire. El libro del cuerpo [The Body Book]. Illustrated by Tony King. Translated by Bertha D. L. de Valverde. México: Editorial Diana, S. A., 1983. 60p. ISBN 968-13-1387-9. $7. Gr. 5-8.
In a direct, explicit, and candid manner, the author explains the functioning of the human body. Simple illustrations accompany the easy-to-understand text that tells about all aspects of the human body. Some readers might object to the frank explanations (and drawings) regarding human sexual intercourse and other biological functions; nonetheless, this is definitely a good introduction for young readers to themselves and their bodies.

Rius, María; J. M. Parramón; and J. J. Puig. El gusto [Taste]. Barcelona: Parramón Ediciones, 1983. [30p.] ISBN 84-342-0331-6. $2.95. Gr. K-2.
Through witty, charming illustrations in color and a

simple text, children learn about the sense of taste. It
discusses good-tasting food (such as cakes, chocolate,
oranges, and honey), sour lemons, salty sea water, and
other flavors. The last two pages offer a scientific and
more detailed explanation of the sense of taste for older
readers. Other titles in this series are La Vista [Sight],
El oído [Ear], El Olfato [Smell], and El Tacto [Touch].

Usborne, Peter, and Su Swallow. Dientes [Teeth]. Bar-
    celona: Editorial Molino, 1981. 24p. ISBN 84-272-5016-9.
    $3. Gr. 1-3.
    For full entry see series title, Biblioteca Educativa In-
    fantil Molino, in Section III.

613.6 PERSONAL SAFETY

Chlad, Dorothy. Cuando hay un incendio sal para afuera
    [When There Is a Fire ... Go Outside]. ISBN 0-516-
    31986-8.

_____. Los desconocidos [Strangers]. ISBN 0-516-31984-1.

    Ea. vol.: 32p. Illustrated by Lydia Halverson. Trans-
    lated by Lada Kratky. (Pueblo de Seguridad). Chicago:
    Childrens Press, 1984. $8.95. Gr. K-2.
    In a simple, easy-to-understand manner, these books
    explain to children what to do in case of a fire in the
    house and how to behave around strangers. The well-
    conceived color illustrations and direct Spanish texts make
    these books excellent safety guides for young children.

613.7 PHYSICAL FITNESS

Usborne, Peter, and Su Swallow. Dormir [Sleep]. Barcelona:
    Editorial Molino, 1981. 24p. ISBN 84-272-5015-0. $3.
    Gr. 1-3.
    For full entry see series title, Biblioteca Educativa In-
    fantil Molino, in Section III.

616.02 FIRST AID

Winch, Brenda. Primeros auxilios [First Aid]. Barcelona:

Marcombo Boixaneu Editores, 1984. 32p. (Biblioteca Técnica Juvenil). ISBN 84-267-0535-9. $8.95. Gr. 6-10.
For full annotation see series title in Section III.

621 APPLIED PHYSICS

Satchwell, John. Como funciona la energía [How Energy
Functions]. Madrid: Editorial Everest, 1982. 41p.
Color photos and drawings. ISBN 84-24-5705-2. $5. Gr.
6-9.
For full entry see series title, Colección Orbita, in Sec-
tion III.

621.388 TELEVISION

Renowden, Gareth. El video [Video]. Barcelona: Marcombo
Boixaneu Editores, 1984. 37p. (Biblioteca Técnica Juvenil).
ISBN 84-267-0522-7. $8.95. Gr. 6-10.
For full annotation see series title in Section III.

623.8 NAUTICAL ENGINEERING AND SEAMANSHIP

Rossiter, Mike. El submarino nuclear [Nuclear Submarine].
Barcelona: Marcombo Boixareu Editores, 1984. 37p. (Biblioteca Técnica Juvenil). ISBN 84-267-0528-6. $8.95. Gr.
6-10.
For full annotation see series title in Section III.

625.1 ENGINEERING OF RAILROADS

Grée, Alain. El metro [The Subway]. Barcelona: Editorial
Juventud, 1981. 29p. ISBN Unavailable. $3. Gr. 4-6.
For full entry see series title, Serie Germán y Ana, in
Section III.

625.7 ENGINEERING OF ROADS AND HIGHWAYS

Usborne, Peter, and Su Swallow. Carreteras [Highways].
Barcelona: Editorial Molino, 1981. 24p. ISBN 84-272-
5004-5. $3. Gr. 1-3.

For full entry see series title, Biblioteca Educativa Infantil Molino, in Section III.

629.13 AERONAUTICS

Chant, Chris. El reactor comercial desde el despegue hasta el aterrizaje [Jetliner from Takeoff to Touchdown]. Barcelona: Marcombo Boixareu Editores, 1984. 37p. (Biblioteca Técnica Juvenil). ISBN 84-267-0521-9. $8.95. Gr. 6-10.
For full annotation see series title in Section III.

Usborne, Peter, and Su Swallow. Aviones [Airplanes]. Barcelona: Editorial Molino, 1981. 24p. ISBN 84-272-5006-1. $3. Gr. 1-3.
For full entry see series title, Biblioteca Educativa Infantil Molino, in Section III.

629.2 MOTOR LAND VEHICLES AND CYCLES

Summer, Philip, and Jenny Tyler. El nacimiento del automóvil [Birth of an Automobile]. Madrid: Ediciones Plesa, 1977. 48p. ISBN 84-7374-029-7. $6. Gr. 6-10.
For full entry see series title, El Museo de los Descubrimentos, in Section III.

Usborne, Peter, and Su Swallow. Automóviles [Automobiles]. Barcelona: Editorial Molino, 1981. 24p. ISBN 84-272-5008-2. $3. Gr. 1-3.
For full entry see series title, Biblioteca Educativa Infantil Molino, in Section III.

Young, Frank. El automóvil [Automobile from Prototype to Scrapyard]. Barcelona: Marcombo Boixareu Editores, 1984. 37p. (Biblioteca Técnica Juvenil). ISBN 84-267-0530-8. $8.95. Gr. 6-10.
For full annotation see series title in Section III.

629.4 ASTRONAUTICS

Behrens, June. Puedo ser astronauta [I Can Be an Astro-
naut] (I Can Be Series). Translated by Lada Kratky.
Chicago: Childrens Press, 1984. 32p. ISBN 0-516-31837-
3. $8.95. Gr. 3-6.
  Excellent photographs in color and an easy-to-understand
text in Spanish explain various aspects of the training astronauts go through before they make their space flights.
Simple illustrations and a glossary add immensely to the
explanations. This is definitely a good introduction to
astronauts for young readers.

629.44 AUXILIARY SPACECRAFT

Friskey, Margaret. Lanzaderas espaciales [Space Shuttles].
Chicago: Childrens Press, 1984. 48p. Photographs,
drawings, index. Translated by Lada Kratky. (Asi es
mi mundo). ISBN 0-516-31655-9. $8.95. Gr. 2-4.
  For full annotation see series title in Section III.

Hawkes, Nigel. La lanzadera espacial [Space Shuttle]. Barcelona: Marcombo Boixareu Editores, 1984. 37p. (Biblioteca Técnica Juvenil). ISBN 84-267-0527-8. $8.95. Gr.
6-10.
  For full annotation see series title in Section III.

630 AGRICULTURE AND RELATED TECHNOLOGIES

La agricultura [Agriculture]. Barcelona: Afha Internacional,
1979. 52p. ISBN Unavailable. $6. Gr. 5-8.
  For full entry see series title, El hombre y su entorno,
in Section III.

631.023 CROPS AND THEIR PRODUCTION,
OCCUPATIONS

Puncel, María. Cuando sea mayor trabajaré en una granja
[When I'm Older, I Will Work on a Farm]. Illustrated by
Letizia Galli. Madrid: Ediciones Altea, 1980. 44p. ISBN
84-372-1418-1. $5. Gr. 5-8.

Despite her protests, a young girl from the city is
sent to live with her aunt and uncle on a farm. Gradually,
she is exposed to many activities that are constantly taking place on a farm: milking cows, shearing sheep, harvesting vegetables and fruits, classifying eggs, and others. She also learns that there are many other duties related to operating a successful farm, such as keeping
records and preparing invoices of products sold. Colorful illustrations of life on a farm complement the simple and
informative text.

633.6 SUGAR CROPS

Giron, Nicole. El azúcar [Sugar]. Illustrated by Ana Villa-
señor. México: Editorial Patria, 1985. 31p. ISBN 968-
39-0099-2. $3. Gr. 3-5.
For full entry see series title, Colección Piñata: Las
materias primas, in Section III.

633.7 ALKALOIDAL CROPS

Vallarta, Luz del Carmen. El chocolate [Chocolate]. Illustrated by Olivia Bond. México: Editorial Patria, 1983.
30p. ISBN 968-39-0057-7. $5. Gr. 3-5.
The origins and the historical and modern uses of chocolate are simply described in a straightforward text. Delightful, colorful illustrations further explain the growing
and various uses of chocolate in Mexico.

634 ORCHARDS, FRUITS, NUTS, FORESTRY

Echeverría, Eugenia. Las frutas [The Fruits]. Illustrated
by Leonel Maciel. México: Editorial Patria, 1981. 40p.
ISBN 96-839-0006-2. $5. Gr. 3-6.
Delightful introduction to many fruits that are grown in
Mexico. A simple, amusing text and spectacular, colorful
illustrations describe about 40 different fruits, emphasizing
their special characteristics.

Noriega, Luisa de. Yo soy el durazno [I Am the Peach].
Illustrated by the author. México: Editorial Trillas, 1983.
24p. ISBN 968-24-1468-7. $3. Gr. 1-3.

The life cycle of a peach is told in a slightly poetic
manner with colorful illustrations. In the beginning there
was a flower that lived happily on a tree, then it became
a green fruit. Eventually the peach was eaten by a little
boy who planted its "heart" amongst the flowers, and a
big tree grew where the birds now sing to the flowers.

634.9 FORESTRY

Saville, Malcolm. El niño quiere saber: explorando un bosque
[The Boy Wants to Know ... Exploring a Forest]. Translated by Jaime Elías Cornet. Illustrated by Elsie Wrigley.
Barcelona: Ediciones Toray, 1982. 32p. ISBN 84-310-
2586-7. $6. Gr. 5-9.
   This is a simple and concise introduction to the many
things that one can find in the woods. It describes the
various types of trees, flowers, plants, insects, birds, and
mammals through brief explanations and unsophisticated illustrations.

636.3 ANIMAL HUSBANDRY, SHEEP AND GOATS

Armellada de Aspe, Virginia. La lana [The Wool]. Illustrated
by Noé Katz. México: Editorial Patria, 1983. 30p. ISBN
968-39-0058-5. $5. Gr. 2-4.
   Through Hilario, a young Mexican shepherd, children
are introduced to the manual process of making serapes:
the caring of sheep, the weaving of the fabric, and the
sewing of the garment. Attractive colorful illustrations of
Mexican rural scenes accompany the simple, direct text.

636.5 POULTRY

Usborne, Peter, and Su Swallow. Huevos [Eggs]. Barcelona:
Editorial Molino, 1981. 24p. ISBN 84-272-5005-3. $3.
Gr. 1-3.
   For full entry see series title, Biblioteca Educativa In-
fantil Molino, in Section III.

636.6 ANIMAL HUSBANDRY, BIRDS OTHER
THAN POULTRY

Prim, Victor, and Helena Rosa. El loro busca casa [The Parrot Seeks a Home]. Barcelona: Editorial Ariel, 1984. 20p. ISBN 84-344-0194-0. $6. Gr. 1-3.
  For full entry see series title, Colección El zoo de los Bibs, in Section III.

636.7 ANIMAL HUSBANDRY, DOGS

Pfloog, Jan. Los perritos son así [What Puppies Are Like]. New York: Random House, 1982. 32p. ISBN 0-394-85604-X. $9. Gr. K-3.
  Brief, simple text and lifelike illustrations tell what puppies are like: they like to chew, bark, play, run, explore, and sleep. Attractive book for dog lovers.

Prim, Victor, and Helena Rosa. El perrito va a la escuela [The Puppy Goes to School]. Barcelona: Editorial Ariel, 1984. 20p. ISBN 84-344-0194-0. $6. Gr. 1-3.
  For full entry see series title, Colección El zoo de los Bibs, in Section III.

Solé Vendrell, Carme. Llivia: pequeña historia de un perro pastor [Llivia: A Short Story of a Sheep Dog]. Barcelona: Ediciones Hymsa, 1982. 24p. ISBN 84-7183-204-6. $4. Gr. 3-5.
  Llivia, a sheep dog, tells about her life as a puppy in the mountains of Spain and later on with a family in Barcelona, Spain. She describes her adaptation to city life as well as her attachment to the family she lives with. Adorable illustrations of Llivia in various predicaments complement the entertaining text.

636.8 ANIMAL HUSBANDRY, CATS

Prim, Victor and Helena Rosa. La Gertrudis tiene gatitos [Gertrudis Has Kittens]. Barcelona: Editorial Ariel, 1984. 20p. ISBN 84-344-0277-0. $6. Gr. 1-3.
  For full entry see series title, Colección El zoo de los Bibs, in Section III.

637 DAIRY AND RELATED TECHNOLOGIES

Usborne, Peter, and Su Swallow. Leche [Milk]. Barcelona:
Editorial Molino, 1981. 24p. ISBN 84-272-5003-7. $3.
Gr. 1-3.
For full entry see series title, Biblioteca Educativa In-
fantil Molino, in Section III.

638 INSECT CULTURE, INCLUDING HONEYBEES

Usborne, Peter, and Su Swallow. Abejas [Bees]. Barcelona:
Editorial Molino, 1981. 24p. ISBN 84-272-5019-3. $3.
Gr. 1-3.
For full entry see series title, Biblioteca Educativa In-
fantil Molino, in Section III.

641.1 APPLIED NUTRITION

Sabugo Pinton, Angel. El libro de la alimentación [Book of
Nutrition]. Illustrated by Constantino Gatagán. León:
Editorial Nebrija, 1980. 76p. ISBN 84-391-2008-7. $7.50.
Gr. 6-9.
For full entry see series title, El libro de la alimenta-
ción, in Section III.

643 HOUSES AND HOUSING EQUIPMENT

Usborne, Peter, and Su Swallow. La casa [Home]. Barcelona:
Editorial Molino, 1981. 24p. ISBN 84-272-5010-X. $3.
Gr. 1-3.
For full entry see series title, Biblioteca Educativa In-
fantil Molino, in Section III.

658.8 MANAGEMENT OF DISTRIBUTION
(Marketing of Goods and Services)

Méndez, Leticia. El mercado [The Market]. Illustrated by
Felipe Ugalde. Colección Piñata, Serie: La Vida Social.
México: Editorial Patria, 1985. 31p. ISBN 968-39-0102-6.
$3. Gr. 3-5.
Flor and her father, Don José, are getting ready for

market day in their nearby town. They sell fruit, clay
pots, and baskets and buy coffee, sugar, salt, and vegetables. Colorful illustrations and a simple text vividly describe a market day in rural Mexico.

Puncel, María. Cuando sea mayor seré comerciante [When
I'm Older, I Will Be a Merchant]. Illustrated by María
Rius. Madrid: Ediciones Altea, 1980. 44p. ISBN 84-
372-1387-8. $5. Gr. 5-8.
   Through the eyes of Ana and Manuel, young readers
are exposed to the life of entrepreneurs. It includes examples of various types of businesses (e.g., a bakery,
pharmacy, grocery store, flower shop) and the problems
associated with running a successful store. It emphasizes
that it is not easy to make money operating a business.
This is a well-conceived introduction to the world of re-
tailing with attractive, colorful illustrations on every
page.

Solano Flores, Guillermo. El mercado [The Market]. Illustrated by Gloria Calderas Lim. México: Editorial Trillas,
1986. 16p. ISBN 968-24-1777-5. $3. Gr. 2-4.
   Shows a boy going to market with his mother. For fuller
entry see series title, Ojos abiertos, in Section III.

676 PULP AND PAPER TECHNOLOGY

Molina, Silvia. El papel [Paper]. Illustrated by Felipe Ugalde.
México: Editorial Partria, 1985. 31p. ISBN 968-39-0081-
X. $3. Gr. 3-5.
   For full entry see series title, Colección Piñata: Las
materias primas, in Section III.

677 SILK PRODUCTION

Corona, Pascuala. La seda [Silk]. Illustrated by the author.
México: Editorial Patria, 1985. 31p. ISBN 968-39-0074-7.
$3. Gr. 3-5.
   For full entry see series title, Colección Piñata, Serie:
Las materias primas, in Section III.

681 MANUFACTURE OF MUSICAL INSTRUMENTS

McLean, Margaret. Construyendo instrumentos musicales
   [Making Musical Instruments]. Barcelona: Marcombo
   Boixareu Editores, 1984. 32p. Biblioteca Técnica Juvenil.
   ISBN 84-267-0536-7. $8.95. Gr. 6-10.
   For full annotation see series title in Section III.

709.72 ART OF MEXICO

Fernández, Justino. El arte mexicano. Middlesex, England:
   Hamlyn House, 1980. 125p. ISBN Unavailable. $11. Gr.
   3-12.
   The great Mexican historian and art critic J. Fernández
   has put together an outstanding example of Mexico's artistic heritage through ceramics, pyramids, sculpture, pal-
   aces, convents, churches, colonial paintings, and modern
   murals. The 59 excellent color photographs show the pre-
   Columbian achievements of the Olmecs, Toltecs, Mayas,
   and Aztecs; the Mexican architecture of the colonial period;
   and, with the Revolution of 1910, the beginnings of Mexican mural painting.

728 RESIDENTIAL BUILDINGS
(Domestic Architecture)

La vivienda [Housing]. Barcelona: Afha Internacional, 1979.
   52p. ISBN Unavailable. $6. Gr. 5-8.
   For full entry see series title, El hombre y su entorno,
   in Section III.

738 CERAMIC ARTS

La cerámica [Ceramics]. Barcelona: Afha Internacional, 1979.
   52p. ISBN Unavailable. $6. Gr. 5-8.
   For fuller entry see series title, El hombre y su entorno,
   in Section III.

738.3 EARTHENWARE AND STONEWARE

Giron, Nicole. El barro [Clay]. Illustrated by Abraham
   Mauricio Salazar. México: Editorial Patria, 1983. 30p.
   ISBN 968-39-0060-7. $5. Gr. 3-5.

The preparation of clay objects in rural Mexico is simply
described for young readers. It tells about the preparation of the clay and the various objects that are made from
clay, such as pots, animal figures, and bricks. Quaint
scenes of rural Mexico accompany each page.

746.6 TEXTILE ART AND HANDICRAFTS-- PRINTING, PAINTING, DYEING

María, Beatriz de, and Campos Castelló. Tres colorantes pre-
hispánicos [Three Prehispanic Dyes]. Illustrated by Pascuala Corona. México: Editorial Patria, 1985. 31p. ISBN
968-39-0100-X. $4. Gr. 3-5.
For full entry see series title, Colección Piñata: Las
materias primas, in Section III.

759.98 HISTORICAL, GEOGRAPHIC TREATMENT OF PAINTING--SOUTH AMERICAN PAINTING

Uribe de Estrada, María Helena, and Elkin Alberto Mesa.
Cecilia Rico: su fauna y su arte primitivo [Cecilia Rico:
Her Animals and Primitive Art]. Illustrated by Cecilia
Rico. Medellín: Editorial Colín, 1982. [52p.] ISBN Unavailable. $5. Gr. 4-Adult.
The purpose of this beautiful book is to attract the attention of children and to expose them to the world of
art. There is no question that the strikingly exotic nature
of these paintings of jungle animals will appeal to children.
Perhaps the text is not what young readers like to read,
but the natural depiction of life in the jungle in various
settings is difficult to describe. The quality of the illustrations is superb. It is unfortunate, however, that the
binding is only glued and thus doesn't hold the pages together.

781.77295 MUSIC COMPOSED OR IMPROVISED IN PUERTO RICO--FOLK MUSIC

Nieves Falcón, Luis. Mi música [My Music]. Illustrated by
Rafael Rivera Rosa. Puerto Rico: Editorial Edil, 1975.
25p. ISBN Unavailable. $3. Gr. 3-6.
Bold, colorful illustrations and easy-to-understand de-

scriptions tell about the musical instruments, dances, songs, and music of Puerto Rico. The historical background as well as interesting information make this a valuable and enjoyable book.

784.6 SONGS FOR SPECIFIC GROUPS AND ON SPECIFIC SUBJECTS

Pahlen, Kurt, and Juan B. Grosso. Música y canciones para los más pequeños [Music and Songs for the Young]. Buenos Aires: Kapelusz, 1973. 80p. ISBN Unavailable. $9. Gr. K-3.
Attractive illustrations and simple songs with music of things common to young children: toys, days of the week, rain, trees, animals, and wind, "Cielito" (Baile argentino, pp. 45-47) is used as an example of a popular Argentine song. The simple vocabulary and short rhythms make this an outstanding addition for young children.

Ribes, Francisco, ed. Canciones de España y América [Spanish and American Songs]. Illustrated by Perellón. Madrid: Santillana, 1965. 84p. ISBN Unavailable. $9. Gr. 1-6.
Fifty-six popular Spanish and Latin American songs and games for children with splendid illustrations have been carefully selected by the editor.

789.9 ELECTRONIC MUSICAL INSTRUMENTS AND MUSIC RECORDING

Bingham, Ken. Manual de grabación: cassettes [Recording Manual: Cassettes]. Madrid: Ediciones Plesa, 1983. 48p. (Colección Electrónica). ISBN 84-7374-110-2. $3.95. Gr. 5-10.
For full annotation see series title in Section III.

790.1 RECREATIONAL ACTIVITIES

Claret, María. Juegos de ayer y de hoy [Games of Yesterday and Today]. Illustrated by the author. Barcelona: Editorial Juventud, 1983. 30p. ISBN 84-261-1923-9. $6.80. Gr. 2-5.

In a touching and amusing manner, the author compares
the games children of today play with the games their
grandparents used to play. Delightful, colorful illustrations and a straightforward text describe children playing
in the snow, playing with clay, jumping rope, flying kites,
playing with hoops, and other games that several genera-
tions of Spanish children have enjoyed.

García Sánchez, José Luis. Los Juegos 1 [Games 1]. Illustrated by José Ramón Sánchez. Valladolid: Editorial
Miñón, 1976. 32p. ISBN 84-355-0466-2. $5. Gr. K-3.
    Charming, colorful illustrations and a simple, brief
text describe games and toys, where children can play,
with whom can they play, and with what can they play.

García Sánchez, José Luis. Los Juegos 2 [Games 2]. Illustrated by José Ramón Sánchez. Valladolid: Editorial
Miñón, 1976. 32p. ISBN 84-355-0467-0. $5. Gr. K-4.
    Witty, colorful illustrations and a brief, simple text
describe various kinds of amusements and games: card
games, chess, ping-pong, fishing, hunting, swimming,
skiing, bowling, gymnastics, motorcycles, pool, dancing,
etc.

García Sánchez, José Luis. Los Juegos 3 [Games 3]. Illustrated by José Ramón Sánchez. Valladolid: Editorial
Miñón, 1976. 32p. ISBN 84-355-0468-9. $5. Gr. K-4.
    Striking, colorful illustrations and a simple, brief text
describe various sports and athletic events: basketball,
boxing, horse races, bicycle riding, car races, soccer,
football, Olympic games, etc.

791.3 CIRCUSES

Ferrán, Jaime. Tarde de circo [Afternoon at the Circus].
Illustrated by Carlos d'Ors. Valladolid: Editorial Miñón,
1982. 97p. ISBN 84-355-0607-X. $7. Gr. 3-6.
    Thirty-four stories in verse and outstanding water-
color illustrations describe an afternoon at the circus. It
tells about clowns, elephants, gymnasts, polar bears,
magicians, acrobats, seals, giraffes, and many other circus activities.

García Sánchez, José Luis. El Circo 1 [The Circus 1]. Illustrated by José Ramón Sánchez. Valladolid: Editorial
Miñón, 1976. 32p. ISBN 84-355-0470-0. $5. Gr. K-2.
   Gorgeous, colorful illustrations and a simple, brief text
describe many people that participate in a circus show:
the director, the orchestra, the chorus girls, strange men
and women, magicians, and clowns.

García Sánchez, José Luis. El Circo 2 [The Circus 2]. Illustrated by José Ramón Sánchez. Valladolid: Editorial
Miñón, 1976. 32p. ISBN 84-355-0471-9. $5. Gr. K-2.
   Circus animals are portrayed in vivid illustrations:
taming lions, tigers, horses, bears, seals, dogs, elephants,
kangaroos, and chimpanzees to be ready to perform for the
circus.

García Sánchez, José Luis. El Circo 3 [The Circus 3]. Illustrated by José Ramón Sánchez. Valladolid: Editorial
Miñón, 1976. 32p. ISBN 84-355-0472-7. $5. Gr. K-2.
   In vivid, colorful illustrations and simple, brief text,
the reader is exposed to the training and skills of various
circus acrobats.

791.43 MOTION PICTURES

Puncel, María. Cuando sea mayor haré cine [When I'm Older,
I Will Make Movies]. Illustrated by Arcadio Lobato. Madrid:
Ediciones Altea, 1979. 45p. ISBN 84-372-1436-X. $5.
Gr. 5-8.
   A young girl relates her experiences in a movie studio.
Her mother needed a make-up assistant, and thus the read-
er learns about various people who are involved in making
movies, such as the director, producer, photographer,
actors, actresses, and others. It emphasizes the hard
work of filmmaking and the importance of good planning.
Amusing illustrations complement the witty and informative
text.

791.5 MINIATURE, TOY, SHADOW THEATERS
(including puppetry)

Hiriart Urdanivia, Berta. Los títeres [Puppets]. Photography

by Marie-Cristine Camus. México: Editorial Patria, 1981.
40p. ISBN 96-839-0001-1. $5. Gr. 3-5.
A young girl describes her life with her family. They
make puppets and produce puppet shows for children. A
simple text and excellent color photographs show the family
at work making puppets, writing stories, setting up a show,
and various other activities involved in producing a puppet
show for children.

792 THEATER (STAGE PRESENTATIONS)

García Sánchez, José Luis. El Teatro 1 [The Theater 1].
Illustrated by José Ramón Sánchez. Valladolid: Editorial
Miñón, 1976. 32p. ISBN 84-355-0473-5. $5. Gr. 3-6.
This is a marvelous introduction to the theater: stage
settings, actors, amusing, sad and romantic scenes, etc.
The brief and simple text and humorous illustrations will
appeal to many young readers.

García Sánchez, José Luis. El Teatro 2 [The Theater 2].
Illustrated by José Ramón Sánchez. Valladolid: Editorial
Miñón, 1976. 32p. ISBN 84-355-0474-3. $5. Gr. 3-6.
Splendid illustrations and a brief, simple text describe
various types of theatrical presentations: Opera, ballet,
drama, verse, mimicry, tragedy, comedy, puppet show,
etc. An interesting appendix briefly discusses five major
playwrights and their works.

García Sánchez, José Luis. El Teatro 3 [The Theater 3].
Illustrated by José Ramón Sánchez. Valladolid: Editorial
Miñón, 1976. 32p. ISBN 84-355-0475-1. $5. Gr. 3-6.
Playful illustrations and a brief, simple text describe
the necessary steps to make a theatrical presentation:
writers, producers, directors, designers, decorators, music, lighting, and the public.

794.8 ELECTRONIC GAMES

Graham, Ian. Juegos de computadoras [Computer Games].
Madrid: Ediciones Plesa, 1983. 48p. (Colección Elec-
trónica). ISBN 84-7374-108-0. $3.95. Gr. 5-10.
For full annotation see series title in Section III.

796.357 BASEBALL

Downing, Joan. El béisbol es nuestro juego [Baseball Is Our
Game]. Translated by Lada Kratky. Photographs: Tony
Freeman. Chicago: Children's Press, 1984. 32p. CIP
ISBN 0-516-33402-6. $8.25. Gr. K-3.
Dynamic, color photographs and simple sentences in
Spanish introduce children to the game of baseball. Books
like this are definitely needed in Spanish book collections
for young readers.

796.4 ATHLETIC EXERCISES AND GYMNASTICS
(including Olympic Games)

Villot, José María. El libro de los deportes olímpicos [Book
of Olympic Sports]. Illustrated by Constantino Gatagan.
León: Editorial Nebrija, 1980. 76p. ISBN 84-391-2007-9.
$8. Gr. 6-12.
There are many facts about Olympic sports reported in
this book, but the most interesting section, which is also
the longest, is the history of the Olympic Games from the
earliest games in 776 B.C. in Greece to the 1980 games in
Moscow. Briefly, it recounts highlights of each game with
eye-catching colorful illustrations. All measurements are
reported in metric, which may be disconcerting to readers
in the U.S. Nonetheless, the topic of this book should
make it appealing to young readers.

808.8 COLLECTIONS FROM MORE THAN
ONE LITERATURE

Belgrano, Margarita, and others. Tío Juan y otros cuentos
[Tío Juan and Other Stories]. Illustrated by Silvina
Martínez and others. Buenos Aires: Centro Editor de
América Latina, 1983? [112p.] ISBN Unavailable. $11.
Gr. 3-5.
The two folktales in this collection of four stories are
indeed appealing: "Chavukú," a Guaraní folktale, tells
how a strong boy became the jaguar; and "El pan de navidad," a European folktale, tells about the beginnings of
fruit cake. The two other stories, unfortunately, are
lethargic and will not interest young readers. Colorful illustrations complement all the stories.

808.83 COLLECTIONS OF FICTION

Andersen, Hans Christian. Cuentos de Andersen [Andersen's Stories]. #1. Madrid: Ediciones Auriga, 1984. 16p. ISBN 84-7281-152-4. $2.95. Gr. 5-8.

Series title: Cuentos de Siempre. Delightful pastel illustrations and a fast-moving text bring out the excitement of such stories as "El patito feo" ("The Ugly Duckling"), "El mechero" ("The Tinderbox"), "Los cisnes salvajes" ("The Wild Swans"), and "La pequeña vendedora de cerillas" ("The Little Match Girl").

Fuertes, Gloria. El dragón tragón [The Dragon Who Ate Too Much]. Illustrated by Sánchez Muñoz. Madrid: Editorial Escuela Española, 1979. 44p. ISBN 84-331-0077-7. $5. Gr. 4-6.

These six witty stories with delightful, colorful illustrations tell about a dragon that was fed up with photographers, an octopus that wanted to be a secretary since he could type and write very fast, a cat from Madrid that found a home for 33 other cats, a small river that became a lake, a little girl who was never afraid, and a magic string of garlic that made wonders for children in school. The author's appealing writing style and sense of words make these especially attractive for reading out loud.

Gesumaría, Susana. El gato de los ojos dorados [The Cat with the Golden Eyes]. Buenos Aires: Aique Grupo Editor, 1980. 63p. ISBN Unavailable. $7. Gr. 6-10.

Three of the five stories included in this book will have a special appeal to teenage girls: "Sietecuernos" tells of a brave girl who gets rid of a gang of obnoxious teenage boys by displaying her talents as a bullfighter: "Espejito, querido espejo" is about the concerns of a 13-year-old girl regarding her own future and her first love; and "Los ojos de Papa Noel" describes Christmas Eve celebrations through the eyes of a mature girl who wanted to protect her little brother from being disappointed with "Papa Noel's" gifts. The other two stories are too ambiguous for young readers. Unfortunately, all of the illustrations are bad; they are uncreative as well as lifeless.

Kincaid, Eric and Lucy, eds. El tesoro de los cuentos [A Treasure of Stories]. Illustrated by the editors. Translated by María Laura Serrano. Buenos Aires: Editorial Sigmar, 1981. 61p. ISBN Unavailable. $8.95. Gr. 4-7.

Spectacular color illustrations accompany these brief, well-written adaptations of the world's best-loved stories. It includes "Puss n' Boots," "Tom Thumb," "Twelve Dancing Princesses," "Aladdin," "Foolish Jack," "A Precious Gift," "The Ugly Duckling," "The Brave Little Tailor," "Jorinda and Joringel," "The Three Spinners," and "The Emperor's New Clothes." This is definitely enjoyable reading.

Osorio, Marta. El último elefante blanco [The Last White Elephant]. Illustrated by Maite Miralles. Valladolid: Editorial Miñón, 1980. 56p. ISBN 84-355-0547-2. $5. Gr. 6-8.

This book contains two fast-moving stories about animals in the Orient (India and Tibet). Both stories are suspenseful and adventurous. "El último elefante blanco" tells about Kamala, a white elephant which grew up in captivity, and Raktamukha, a vagabond monkey. They became good friends and together found a way to free Kamala, take him back to the forest where he was born, and allow him to live a normal life with other grey elephants. "El aguilucho" is about Nan Singh, a kind-hearted monk, and Kang Rimpoche, a young eagle. Nan Singh saved Kang Rimpoche from two hunters who were going to kill her and cared for her during her early years. When they had to part, they still remained close and helped each other whenever they were in danger.

These well-written stories will entertain young readers with their exciting plots and adorable characters. The black-and-white illustrations convey very well Indian and Tibetan moods.

Patience, John. La búsqueda del tesoro [Parson Dimby's Treasure Hunt]; Líos en la mansión [Muddles at the Manor]. Illustrated by the author. Translated by J. M. Pérez Miguel. Madrid: Editorial Everest, 1984. [36p.] ISBN 84-241-5273-5. $6.50. Gr. 3-5.

These stories tell about two exciting happenings in the town of Valdehelechos: La búsqueda del tesoro shows how

slow Moli Púas was the distinguished winner in Parson
Dimly's treasure hunt. Líos en la mansión tells about rabbit, the gardener, and his experiences in trying to be especially creative in the mansion's garden. Like the previous books in this series, gorgeous, colorful illustrations
of animals at work and at play complement both stories.

Patience, John. El inofensivo espantapájaros. La sorpresa
del cumpleaños de Salomón [The Inoffensive Scarecrow.
Salomon's Birthday Surprise]. Illustrated by the author.
Translated by J. M. Pérez Miguel. León: Editorial Everest, 1984. 41p. ISBN 84-241-5274-3. $7. Gr. 3-5.
   Both of these lighthearted stories tell about the lives
of animals and their amusing predicaments. El inofensivo
espantapájaros shows a busy farmer and his family trying
to get rid of nasty crows. After many unsuccessful attempts, Papa Badger invented an automatic whistling scarecrow, which finally scared the crows away. La sorpresa
del cumpleaños de Salomón tells about a mix-up which re-
sulted in a strange birthday gift. Uncle Oscar confused
the labels on two packages and inadvertently sent a huge
crocodile to his nephew and a box of honey to the zoo.
Colorful illustrations of animals in various situations add
cheerfulness to the buoyant text.

Patience, John. Olimpíada en Valdehelechos [Olympics in
Valdehelechos]. Illustrated by the author. Translated by
J. M. Pérez Miguel. Madrid: Editorial Everest, 1982.
41p. ISBN 84-241-5272-7. $7. Gr. 3-5.
   Two stories are included in this volume. "Olimpíada en
Valdehelechos" describes the town's excitement, disappoint-
ment, and subsequent animation due to the celebration of
sports' day in Valdehelechos, a small town in the middle of
a forest. "La nueva casa del señor Robin" tells about the
problems in the Robin family's old house and how, with the
help of their new friends, they built a beautiful new house.
Gorgeous, colorful illustrations of life-like animals at work
and at play complement both stories.

Patience, John. El señor Tejoncito, globonauta. Ladrones
en Valdehelechos [Mr. Badger the Balloonist. Robbers in
Valdehelechos]. Illustrated by the author. Translated by

J. M. Pérez Miguel. León: Editorial Everest, 1982. 41p.
ISBN 84-241-5271-9. $7. Gr. 3-5.

There are many things going on in the little town of
Valdehelechos. These two stories tell, in an amusing and
lighthearted manner, what happens when mister Tejoncito
(Mister Badger) unexpectedly decides to fly his hot-air
balloon over the town of Valdehelechos and how two robbers were caught after they stole a big brass drum and a
horn from the house of Mr. Ricomarqués. Colorful, witty
illustrations add a joyous tone to these entertaining stories
originally published in England.

Walsh, María Elena. Chaucha y Palito [Chaucha and Palito].
Illustrated by Vilar. Buenos Aires: Editorial Sudamericana, 1977. 169p. ISBN Unavailable. $8. Gr. 5-9.

The author's marvelous, witty, alluring style will delight readers in this collection of science-fiction stories,
including stories about a castle in the sky; Felipito, who
was anxious to become a "gaucho"; a group of fifth graders
who saved a colony of octopi by giving them all their hair;
a huge iguana that gained the affection of a poor family;
and the amazing love story between Aniceta and a colonel.
However, the best part of this book is the author's auto-
biography, which comprises the last 18 pages. In it,
María Elena Walsh relates her years as a child and adolescent in Buenos Aires, her travels to New York and Europe,
and important incidents which affected her professional and
personal development. Amusing illustrations complement
the text.

861 SPANISH POETRY

Arribillaga, Manuelita. ¡Liralirón! [Liraliron!]. Illustrated
by Leticia Uhalde. Buenos Aires: Editorial Plus Ultra,
1978. 47p. ISBN Unavailable. $5. Gr. 2-4.

Eighteen simple, lively rhymes about things common to
children. It includes rhymes about animals, toys, and
games. The unaffected language used in these rhymes
will certainly appeal to children. Unfortunately, the illustrations do not do much for each rhyme; they are merely
three-tone lifeless decorations.

Bertolino, Roberto. Ayer [Yesterday]. Illustrated by Ale-
jandro Terrera. Buenos Aires: Editorial Plus Ultra, 1978.
47p. ISBN Unavailable. $5. Gr. 5-12.

This is a simple and poetic narrative which describes
the author's feelings about why "yesterday" will live forever in his heart. The child-like cover and illustrations
might deceive some readers into believing that this is a
picture book for young children, but its tender, abstract
thoughts will have more meaning to older readers. Here
is an example: "Había una vez un pedazo, de tiempo que
se llamaba Ayer.... Parecía el más grande y el más her-
moso del mundo.... Porque uníamos las distancias con
recuerdos." ["Once upon a time there was a piece of time
that was called Yesterday ... It looked like the greatest
and the most beautiful one in the world ... Because we
united distances with memories."] (pp. 8, 10, 38).

Fuertes, Gloria. El libro loco de todo un poco: libro primero
[A Crazy Book: A Little Bit About Everything]. Illustrated by Ulises Wensell. Madrid: Editorial Escuela Española, 1984. 45p. ISBN 84-331-0124-2. $4.95. Gr. 3-
5.

In an amusing and light-hearted manner, these poems
describe a visit to the zoo, a meal at a restaurant, two
ladies talking about a dog, the dance of a spider, and other playful situations. Jovial, colorful illustrations are a
perfect complement to "this crazy book."

Kruse, Lily. Barquitos de papel [Little Paper Boats]. Illustrated by Franco Céspedes. San José: Universidad
Autónoma de Centro América, 1982. 98p. ISBN Unavailable. $9. Gr. 3-5.

Sixty-five light-hearted poems for children are included
in this collection. There are poems about flowers, animals,
toys, grandmother, and other things common to children.
The naturalness of the language makes these poems a joy
to listen to or to read. The two-tone illustrations, unfortunately, lack the spontaneity of the poems.

Luján, Fernando. Poemas para niños: antología [Anthology of
Children's Poems]. Illustrated by Francisco Amighetti.
San José: Editorial Costa Rica, 1982. 88p. ISBN Unavail-
able. $4. Gr. 6-10.

Thirty poets of Latin America and Spain are represented
in this anthology of 74 poems and nursery rhymes about
the sea, games and songs, animals, flowers, and countryside. Some of the poets included are Pablo Antonio Cuadra,
Fernando Luján, Miguel de Unamuno, Gabriela Mistral, and
Federico García Lorca. Insipid two-tone engravings do not
do justice to the poems.

Medina, Arturo, editor. El silbo del aire--antología lírica
infantil [Anthology of Children's Lyrics]. Barcelona:
Vicens-Vives, 1979. Vol. I, 108p.; Vol. II, 136p. ISBN
84-316-0096-9; 84-316-0099-3. $9. Gr. K-3 and 3-8.
    Volume I, for the younger children, contains gorgeous
illustrations of simple poems, nursery rhymes, songs, riddles and games. Some of the authors represented are
Rafael Alberti, Gloria Fuertes, Antonio Machado, Amado
Nervo, and Lope de Vega. Volume II, for grades 3 to 8,
contains beautiful illustrations of narrative poems for older
children. Some of the authors represented are García
Lorca, Juan Ramón Jiménez, Antonio Machado, and Gabriela
Mistral.

Romero, Marina. Alegrías--poemas para niños [Happiness--
Poems for Children]. Illustrated by Sigfrido de Guzmán
y Gimeno. Salamanca: Anaya, 1972. 146p. ISBN 84-
207-0884-4. $13. Gr. K-2.
    Outstanding illustrations and simple poems of things
which delight children, such as Peter Pan, Pinocchio, a
fox, an ostrich, a macaw, a pigeon, and others.

Walsh, María Elena. Tutú Marambá [Tutú Marambá]. Buenos
Aires: Editorial Sudamericana, 1984. 97p. ISBN 95-007-
0141-3. $9. Gr. 3-6.
    Outstanding collection of simple poems and rhymes of
things common to all children: toys, animals, friends, and
others. Attractive line illustrations, witty situations, and
simple vocabulary will be enjoyed by all children. Some
examples are "El vendedor de sueños" (p. 34), "Pájaro
loco" (p. 38), and "Nada más" (p. 56).

Walsh, María Elena. Zoo loco [Crazy Zoo]. Buenos Aires:
Editorial Sudamericana, 1970. 18p. ISBN Unavailable. $3.
Gr. 3-6.

Excellent short limericks with simple vocabulary and appealing illustrations about zoo animals. A few pertain di-
rectly to Argentina, which make them an excellent introduction to that country. Others discuss animals in Ecuador
and around Caracas, but most show animals that all children know.

862 PLAYS IN SPANISH

Vázquez-Vigo, Carmen. Jugar al teatro [Playing Theater].
Illustrated by Ma. Jesús Fernández Castillo. Madrid:
Editorial Miñón, 1984. 73p. ISBN 84-355-0676-2. $4.
Gr. 4-6.
These two brief plays to encourage children to play theater are written in a lighthearted, natural style. "Prin-
cesas y fantasmas" shows how two brothers and two sisters
become princesses and ghosts just after having had measles.
"Corazón de reloj" tells how a superstitious, miserly, cold-
hearted, old man becomes a kind dancer who gives out
candy to children. Amusing black-and-white line illustrations add interest to the text.

863 SPANISH FICTION

Cervantes Saavedra, Miguel de. Aventuras de Don Quijote
de la Mancha [Adventures of Don Quijote de la Mancha].
Adapted by Joaquín Aguirre Bellver. Illustrated by C.
Perellón. Madrid: Edaf, 1972. 108p. ISBN Unavailable.
$9. Gr. 5-12.
The enchanting dialogue and original humor of Cervantes'
Don Quijote has been maintained in this superb adaptation
with beautiful illustrations of Don Quijote's adventures.

Gefaell, María Luisa. El Cid [The Cid]. Illustrated by Laszlo
Gal. Barcelona: Noguer, 1970. 135p. ISBN 84-279-3201-4.
$13. Gr. 3-12.
The life and philosophy of the famous twelfth-century
Spanish knight, Don Rodrigo Díaz de Vivar, is magnificent-
ly illustrated in this handsome adaptation of the famous
Spanish epic poem. There are splendid illustrations of
Spanish feudal cities, kings, and battles.

Samaniego, Felix María. Fábulas [Fables]. Barcelona: Veron,
1975. 168p. ISBN 84-7255-068-0. $15. Gr. 4-12.
Fascinating collection of the famous eighteenth-century
fables which should charm all Spanish-speakers. It includes
excellent short fables with handsome illustrations.

Samaniego, Félix de. Mis fábulas [My Fables]. Illustrated by
Carlos A. Chapman I. Caracas: R. J. Ediciones, 1984.
[12p.] ISBN Unavailable. $3. Gr. 3-6.
Seven of Samaniego's delightful fables are included in
this sturdy publication. Unfortunately, the cartoon-like
illustrations cannot compare to other published versions of
these fables.

863.008 COLLECTION OF FICTION BY
SPANISH AUTHORS

Bravo-Villasante, Carmen. El libro de las fábulas [Book of
Fables]. Illustrated by Carmen Andrada. Valladolid:
Editorial Miñón, 1982. 104p. ISBN 84-355-0634-7. $8.
Gr. 6-12.
Sixty-three fables written by well-known authors from
Spain, Argentina, Colombia, Cuba, Mexico, Nicaragua,
Peru, Santo Domingo, San Salvador, and Venezuela are in-
cluded in this collection which will delight fluent Spanish-
speakers. Unfortunately, the awkward illustrations do not
do justice to the innate wit of these fables.

867 SPANISH SATIRE AND HUMOR

Capdevila, Roser. ¡Eh! no me dejéis sol [Hey! Don't Leave
Me Sun]. Barcelona: Ediciones Destino, 1985. [46p.]
ISBN 84-233-1375-1. $5. Gr. 5-Adult.
Readers of all ages will be enthralled by this delightfully witty account of the sun's activities on the earth.
Amusing, pastel illustrations and one sentence per page
describe how the sun fills the earth with light and warmth.
For example, the sun wishes to continue to spy on bored
executives, to make Aunt Rosario sweat while jogging, to
snoop through half-closed windows, and many other human
activities. This book is dedicated to the rulers of the world--
older readers may get the political message; younger readers will enjoy it.

897.1 POETRY OF NORTH AMERICAN
NATIVE LANGUAGES

Gerez, Toni de. Mi canción es un pedazo de jade: poemas del México antiguo [My Song Is a Piece of Jade: Ancient Mexican Poems]. Illustrated by Guillermo Stark. México: Editorial Novaro, 1984. 48p. ISBN 96-848-0015-0. $5. Gr. 6-10.

This is an outstanding collection of Nahuatl poems from pre-Columbian Mexico that have been beautifully adapted/ translated by Toni de Gerez with striking pre-Columbian-type illustrations. This is an excellent introduction to pre-Columbian culture, gods, and literature which will interest most readers with its splendid thoughts and wisdom.

909 WORLD HISTORY

Manley, Deborah. Es divertido descubrir el pasado [It Is Fun to Discover the Past]. Illustrated by Moira and Colin Maclean, Kailer-Lowndes, and Sally Gregory. Barcelona: Plaza y Janés, 1983. 61p. ISBN 84-01-70155-4. $6. Gr. 5-8.

Through colorful illustrations and a brief text, young readers are exposed to the past. It tells about dinosaurs; cavemen; ancient Egypt, Greece, and Rome; agriculture; China; primitive machines; history of aviation; early trains; cowboys; and other topics. Good introduction to world history for reluctant readers.

Middleton, Haydn. El siglo XVI [Everyday Life in the Sixteenth Century]. ISBN 84-272-5971-9.

Taylor, Laurence. El siglo XVII [Everyday Life in the Seventeenth Century]. ISBN 84-272-5972-7.

Grant, Neil. El siglo XVIII [Everyday Life in the Eighteenth Century]. ISBN 84-272-5973-5.

Chamberlin, E. R. El siglo XIX [Everyday Life in the Nineteenth Century]. ISBN 84-272-5974-3.

Ea. vol.: 61p. Color illustrations. (Pueblos del Pasado). Barcelona: Editorial Molino, 1984. $5. Gr. 5-10.

Through outstanding maps, charts, color illustrations,
well-known paintings of each period, photographs and a
readable text, readers are introduced to a great civilization. Each book is divided into brief chapters that describe significant events, transportation, the family, clothing, agriculture, law and order, health and medicine, education, religion, recreation, scientific achievements, important cities, and others. In addition, each book contains
a chronology of events and a list of important people. This
is definitely an excellent series to introduce world history
to young readers. Other titles in this series are Egipcios,
Griegos, Romanos, Vikingos, Aztecas, Normandos, Celtas,
Incas, Sajones, Chinos.

912 GRAPHIC REPRESENTATIONS OF THE EARTH'S SURFACE INCLUDING MAP READING

Quiero saber sobre ... los mapas [I Want to Know About ...
Maps]. Illustrated by Carlos A. Chapman I. Caracas:
R. J. Ediciones, 1984? 12p. ISBN Unavailable. $3. Gr.
3-5.
Through the ingenuity of eight-year-old Yamanuy, a
brave and smart Indian boy, children learn about the advantages of maps. It also includes a brief history of maps
as well as an introduction to interpreting maps. This is
not an in-depth study of maps, but rather an amusing introduction to them, along with colorful illustrations.

930 GENERAL HISTORY OF ANCIENT WORLD

Caselli, Giovanni. El imperio romano y la Europa medieval
[The Roman Empire and the Dark Ages]. 48p. ISBN 84-
7525-250-8.

_____. Las primeras civilizaciones [The First Civilizations].
48p. ISBN 84-7525-249-4.

Connolly, Peter. La vida en tiempos de Jesús de Nazareth
[Living in the Times of Jesus of Nazareth]. 96p. ISBN
84-7525-230-3.

Ea. vol.: (La Vida en el Pasado). Madrid: Ediciones
Generales Anaya. 1895. $13. Gr. 6-10.

Through excellent charts, maps, illustrations, and photographs in color and a simple text, readers are introduced to the history of humanity. Each volume emphasizes the customs, daily life, and common objects used by the people in the different historical eras. El imperio romano y la Europa medieval describes the Roman Empire from the times of the Celts in the year 50 B.C. until the fourteenth century. Las primeras civilizaciones introduces readers to man of the Stone Age up to the ancient Greeks. La vida en tiempos de Jesús de Nazareth reconstructs life in Palestine from the time of King Herod up to the destruction of the Temple in Jerusalem and the end of Judea.

930.1 ARCHAEOLOGY

La arqueología [Archeology]. Barcelona: Afha Internacional, 1979. 52p. ISBN Unavailable. $6. Gr. 5-8.
    For fuller entry see series title, El hombre y su entorno, in Section III.

936 HISTORY OF ANCIENT WORLD
(Europe North and West of Italian Peninsula to 499)

Stahel, Hans R. Nacimiento de un palafito [Birth of a Prehistoric Village]. Barcelona: Timum Mas, 1981. 72p. ISBN 84-7176-392-3. $6. Gr. 6-9.
    The origins and lifestyle of a town of prehistoric lake dwellers are interestingly depicted through a readable text and simple black-and-white line illustrations. These amazing towns constructed of wood above water were developed in Europe in approximately 5000 B.C. The author discusses the people's occupations, houses, utensils, food, artworks, toys, and other aspects of their lives.

946 HISTORY OF SPAIN

Ionescu, Angela C. La misma piedra [The Same Stone]. Illustrated by Javier Serrano Pérez. Madrid: Editorial Doncel, 1981. 134p. ISBN 84-325-0381-9. $9. Gr. 6-9.
    Through the fantasies and games of an Iberian boy and a boy from modern Spain, young readers are introduced to the diverse cultures and races that have lived in Spain

throughout the centuries. This is a clever and simple introduction to the history of Spain with appropriate illustrations in color.

949.4 SWITZERLAND

Bonnardel, Rene. Lionel y los animales de la montaña [Lionel and the Mountain Animals]. Bilbao: Editorial Fher, 1980. 28p. ISBN 84-243-1392-5. $4.50. Gr. 5-8.
For full entry see series title, Los niños y animales, in Section III.

964 SAHARA

Tondeur, Freddy. Slimane y los animales del desierto [Slimane and the Desert Animals]. Bilbao: Editorial Fher, 1980. 28p. Color Photos. ISBN 84-243-1388-7. $4.50. Gr. 5-8.
For full entry see series title, Los niños y los animales, in Section III.

972 MEXICO

Jacobsen, Karen. México [Mexico]. Chicago: Childrens Press, 1984. 48p. Photographs, drawings, index. Translated by Lada Kratky. (Así es mi mundo). ISBN 0-516-31632-X. $8.95. Gr. 2-4.
For full annotation see series title in Section III.

Urrutia, Cristina, and Marcial Camilo. El maíz [Corn]. Illustrated by Marcial Camilo. México: Editorial Patria, 1981. 44p. ISBN 96-839-0004-6. $5. Gr. 3-5.
Life in rural Mexico is beautifully described through the planting, harvesting, and cooking of corn. Stunning water-color illustrations and a simple text show how corn is grown, life in a village, celebrating a good harvest, working on the fields, and many other activities related to the eating and growing of corn in Mexico.

972.93 DOMINICAN REPUBLIC

Moya Pons, Frank. Historia Dominicana para niños [Dominican
History for Children]. Santo Domingo: Por el autor, 1979.
85p. ISBN Unavailable. $5. Gr. 5-8.
   Succinctly, the author narrates the history of the Do-
minican Republic, beginning with the discovery of the island
up to its independence in 1844. The brevity of each chap-
ter and the carefully selected two-tone illustrations and
maps make this an adequate historical narrative.

972.95 PUERTO RICO

Alegría, Ricardo E. Descubrimiento, conquista y colonización
de Puerto Rico [Discovery, Conquest, and Colonization of
Puerto Rico]. Spain: Colección de Estudios Puertorriqueños, 1975. 175p. ISBN Unavailable. $8. Gr. 6-12.
   Excellent introduction to the discovery, conquest, and
colonization of Puerto Rico written in a simple, easy-to-
understand text. It also includes outstanding color and
black-and-white reproductions of paintings, maps, and
drawings that greatly enhance the readers' interest of the
fifteenth and sixteenth centuries of life in Puerto Rico and
Europe.

La Brucherie, Roger A. Imágenes de Puerto Rico [Images of
Puerto Rico]. El Centro, California: Imágenes Press,
1985. [148p.] ISBN 0-939302-12-8. $21.95. Gr. 6-Adult.
   Spectacular photographs in color are the basis of this
photographic-essay on Puerto Rico, which includes chapters
on the history, heritage, "jíbaro," the island, "New" San
Juan, today in Puerto Rico, natural resources, and Old
San Juan. The author does not pretend to offer an in-
depth analysis of Puerto Rican history, culture, or society
but rather a verbal and visual collection of personal impressions and observations which he gathered during the
five months that he spent on the island. Hence, this book
reflects the author's subjective interpretations of Puerto
Rico's past, present, and future. Unfortunately, it does
not contain a table of contents nor an index which may
limit its use for those desiring specific information on
Puerto Rico. Notwithstanding these limitations, this is a
gorgeous visual panorama of Puerto Rico. (This book is
also available in English.)

972.95004 NATIVE RACES IN PUERTO RICO

Alegría, Ricardo E. Historia de nuestros indios (versión elemental) [History of Our Indians]. Illustrated by Mela Pons de Alegría. San Juan de Puerto Rico: Universidad, 1982. 86p. ISBN Unavailable. $8. Gr. 3-5.

In simple text and easy-to-read explanations, the reader is introduced to the history of the Indians of Puerto Rico. This book, originally published in 1969, includes the discovery of the Indians, their origins, furniture, housing, family, dress government, religion, fishing, hunting, transportation, games, war, and heritage. Unfortunately, the insipid two-tone illustrations do not add much interest to the historical narrative.

973 UNITED STATES

Anno, Mitsumasa. El viaje de Anno IV [Anno's USA]. Barcelona: Editorial Juventud, 1983. [48p.] ISBN 84-261-2006-7. $11.95. Gr. 3-7.

Through Anno's beautifully, detailed illustrations, young readers are exposed to scenes of U.S. history, art, literature, folklore, and lifestyles. This wordless panorama of the U.S. is the last one of this series now published in Spain. Previous titles are El viaje de Anno I--Europa del Norte [Anno's Journey], El viaje de Anno II--Italia [Anno's Italy], El viaje de Anno III--Inglaterra [Anno's Britain].

Krueger, Bonnie, and Martine Steltzer. Vivir en Estados Unidos [Living in the United States]. Photography by Laurence Vidal. Madrid: Editorial Everest, S. A., 1980. 64p. ISBN 84-241-5662-5. $8. Gr. 5-10.

The greatness and diversity of people and life in the U.S., as viewed by many Europeans, are depicted in this book with outstanding color and black-and-white photographs. Perhaps some readers will object to what seems to be the authors' overemphasis of prejudice in American society; nevertheless, they also describe the optimism and hope prevalent in many aspects of life in the U.S.

982 ARGENTINA

Guait, Camilo. Furia de oro en el Páramo [Gold Rush at the

Páramo].   Illustrated by Blas Alfredo Castagna.   Buenos
Aires: Ediciones Toqui, 1977.   42p.   ISBN Unavailable.
$5.   Gr. 6-10.

The fast-moving text and striking black-and-white illustrations tell the story of the gold rush era in the
southernmost part of Argentina in the 1880's.   It relates
well-known episodes of an unusual war between Julio Pop-
per, a Rumanian gold prospector, and many adventures in
search of gold.   Young readers will experience the adventures, dangers, and excitement which prevailed in Argentina before the establishment of the large farming estates.

Guait, Camilo.   Viaje al país de las manzanas [Journey to the
Land of Apples].   Illustrated by Jeremías Sanyú.   Buenos
Aires: Aique Grupo Editor, S.R.L., 1981.   47p.   ISBN
Unavailable. $5.   Gr. 6-9.

George Musters, an Englishman by birth and also known
as the "South American Marco Polo," explored the unknown
Patagonian region in 1869 and 1870 accompanied by the
Tehuelche Indians.   This fast-paced adventure story relates the dangers and excitement of that trip, which included hunger, an inhospitable desert, wild animals, and
hostile Indian tribes.   Unfortunately, the coarse black-and-
white illustrations do not equal the excitement of the story.

985 PERU

Millard, Anne.   Los incas [The Incas].   Translated by Norma
Huidobro.   Illustrated by Richard Hook.   Buenos Aires:
Editorial Sigmar, 1981.   44p.   ISBN Unavailable. $5.   Gr.
6-10.

The splendor and achievements of the Inca civilization
are magnificently portrayed through excellent color photographs and drawings and a straightforward text.   It describes the life of the emperor and his nobles, the organization of the empire, the Incas' amazing building skills, the
beautiful crafts produced by the people living in the Andes,
as well as many other aspects of Inca civilization.   This
book is a marvelous introduction to the Inca empire which
"was built in the 15th century and lasted less than a hundred years."

987 VENEZUELA

Pipo Kilómetro viaja por Venezuela. Primera parte [Pipo
    Kilometer Travels Through Venezuela, Part 1]. Caracas:
    Cromotip, 1980? 40p. ISBN Unavailable. $5. Gr. 3-5.
    Pipo, a young Venezuelan boy, embarks on an imaginary
trip to see his country. A simple text and pleasing watercolor illustrations show Pipo flying on a kite over Mara-
caibo; arriving at the port of La Guaira; waking up in
Pertigalete, where there is a huge cement factory; walking
on the streets of Caracas, the capital, with its traffic and
pollution; and visiting mountains, valleys, and small towns
of Venezuela. (This story continues in Part II, below.)
There is a simple map of Venezuela on the last page of
this volume. This is certainly a most appealing introduction to the geography of Venezuela.

Pipo Kilómetro viaja por Venezuela. Segunda parte [Pipo
    Kilometer Travels Through Venezuela, Part 2]. Caracas:
    Cromotip, 1980? 34p. ISBN Unavailable. $5. Gr. 3-5.
    Pipo continues on his imaginary trip through Venezuela
(see entry above). This time he goes by vast forests;
beautiful fields; the great Orinoco River; huge dams that
produce electricity; and Salto Angel, the world's highest
waterfall. He also meets two Indians who help him cross
the river in a canoe, and he sees a few animals--herons
and turtles--that inhabit Venezuela. As in Part I, this
volume also has a simple text and attractive watercolor illustrations. As previously stated, this is a most appealing
introduction of the geography of Venezuela.

92 BIOGRAPHY OF INDIVIDUALS

Alavedra, José. La extraordinaria vida de Pablo Casals [The
    Extraordinary Life of Pablo Casals]. Barcelona: Ayma,
    1969. 121p. ISBN 84-209-2085-1. $8. Gr. 6-12.
    The artistic development of this great Spanish cellist is
exquisitely portrayed by the author, who knew Casals very
well. It describes Casals' youth, his musical education in
Barcelona, Madrid and Paris, and his successes as a master
cellist and composer. Very little mention is made of Casals'
wife, Martita.

92B INDIVIDUAL BIOGRAPHY

García Barquero, Juan Antonio. Juan Sebastián Bach [Johann
Sebastian Bach]. 73p. ISBN 84-241-5425-8.

Morán, Francisco José. Leonardo da Vinci [Leonardo da Vinci].
57p. ISBN 84-241-5428-2.

Morán, Francisco José. Pablo Ruiz Picasso [Pablo Ruiz Picas-
so]. 57p. ISBN 84-241-5429-0.

 Ea. vol.: Color photographs. (Grandes Hombres).
Madrid: Editorial Everest, 1984. $5.50. Gr. 6-12.
 The excellent quality of these books should serve to entice readers into the worlds of music and art as exemplified
by these masters. Each book includes outstanding color
photographs that compliment the discussion of the life,
works, and times of these artists. The most readable of
these books is Picasso's biography. It tells about Picasso's
early life, travels, romantic involvements, and successes in
the arts. The color reproductions of Picasso's masterpieces
further add to the enjoyment of this book. Leonardo da
Vinci's and Bach's biographies are written in a more com-
plex, philosophical style which may not appeal to readers
unfamiliar with the works of these artists. Nevertheless,
the outstanding color reproductions of Leonardo da Vinci's
masterpieces and of Bach's contemporaries, as well as the
wealth of information about these two great artists make
these books welcome additions to many collections.

- SECTION III: PUBLISHERS' SERIES

ASI ES MI MUNDO

363.2

Broekel, Ray. La policía [Police]. ISBN 0-516-31643-5.

567.9

Clark, Mary Lou. Dinosaurios [Dinosaurs]. ISBN 0-516-
31612-5.

629.44

Friskey, Margaret. Lanzaderas espaciales [Space Shuttles].
ISBN 0516-31655-9.

972

Jacobsen, Karen. México [Mexico]. ISBN 0516-31632-X.

523

Lewellen, John. La luna, el sol, y las estrellas [Moon, Sun
and Stars]. ISBN 0516-31637-0.

   Ea. vol.: 48p. Photographs, drawings, index. Translated by Lada Kratky. (Así es mi mundo). Chicago:
Childrens Press, 1984. $8.95. Gr. 2-4.
   This is a well-done Spanish translation of the "New True
Books" series which exposes children to high-interest topics on science and social studies. A straightforward, easy-
to-read Spanish text and vivid, color photographs or illustrations introduce children to the activities of the police,

to a number of different dinosaurs, to the operation and
uses of reusable space vehicles, to Mexico and its people,
and to the relationship between the moon, the earth, and
the sun. The paucity of simple, nonfiction books in Spanish makes this series a highly desirable one for young
Spanish-speaking readers.

BIBLIOTECA EDUCATIVA INFANTIL MOLINO

                          551.57

Usborne, Peter, and Su Swallow. Lluvia [Rain]. ISBN 84-
   272-5001-0.

_____, and _____. Nieve [Snow]. ISBN 84-272-5012-6.

                          363.3

_____, and _____. Fuego [Fire]. ISBN 84-272-5002-9.

                          637

_____, and _____. Leche [Milk]. ISBN 84-272-5003-7.

                          625.7

_____, and _____. Carreteras [Highways]. ISBN 84-
   272-5004-5.

                          636.5

_____, and _____. Huevos [Eggs]. ISBN 84-272-5005-3.

                          629.13

_____, and _____. Aviones [Airplanes]. ISBN 84-272-
   5006-1.

                          523.3

_____, and _____. La luna [Moon]. ISBN 84-272-
   5007-X.

629.2

_____, and _____. Automóviles [Automobiles]. ISBN 84-272-5008-8.

598

_____, and _____. Aves [Birds]. ISBN 84-272-5009-6.

643

_____, and _____. La casa [House]. ISBN 84-272- 5010-X.

523.7

_____, and _____. El sol [Sun]. ISBN 84-272-5011-8.

385

_____, and _____. Trenes [Trees]. ISBN 84-272-5013-4.

535.6

_____, and _____. Color [Color]. ISBN 84-272-5014-2.

613.7

_____, and _____. Dormir [Sleep]. ISBN 84-272-5015-0.

612

_____, and _____. Dientes [Teeth]. ISBN 84-272- 5016-9.

391

_____, and _____. Vestidos [Dress]. ISBN 84-272- 5017-7.

582.16

_____, and _____. Arboles [Trees]. ISBN 84-272- 5018-5.

638

_____, and _____. Abejas [Bees]. ISBN 84-272-5019-3.

Ea. vol.: 24p. (Biblioteca Educativa Infantil Molino).
Barcelona: Editorial Molino, 1981. $3. Gr. 1-3.
These 19 books provide basic information about common
things described in each title. Simple texts and illustrations make these books excellent introductions to common
elements, things, or animals for young children.

BIBLIOTECA TECNICA JUVENIL

629.13

Chant, Chris. El reactor comercial desde el despegue hasta
el aterrizaje [Jetliner from Takeoff to Touchdown]. 37p.
ISBN 84-267-0529-4.

004

Graham, Ian. El ordenador [Computer]. 37p. ISBN 84-
267-0521-9.

629.44

Hawkes, Nigel. La lanzadera espacial [Space Shuttle]. 37p.
ISBN 84-267-0527-8.

681

McLean, Margaret. Construyendo instrumentos musicales
[Making Musical Instruments]. 32p. ISBN 84-267-0536-7.

581

Pavord, Anna. Botánica recreativa [Growing Things]. 32p.
ISBN 84-267-0537-5.

621.388

Renowden, Gareth. El video [Video]. 37p. ISBN 84-267-
0522-7.

623.8

Rossiter, Mike. El submarino nuclear [Nuclear Submarine].
37p. ISBN 84-267-0528-6.

629.2

Young, Frank. El autómovil [Automobile from Prototype to
Scrapyard]. 37p. ISBN 84-267-0530-8.

508

Wicks, Keith. Ciencia recreativa [Science Can Be Fun].
32p. ISBN 84-267-0538-3.

616.02

Winch, Brenda. Primeros auxilios [First Aid]. 32p. ISBN
84-267-0535-9.

Ea. vol.: (Biblioteca Técnica Juvenil). Barcelona:
Marcombo Boixareu Editores, 1984. $8.95. Gr. 6-10.
The purpose of this series is to introduce young readers to the world of technology or to encourage them into
new hobbies or activities. Simple explanations and illustrations are the main attributes of this series. All titles
were originally published in Great Britain.

LA BRUJULA

523

Dultzin, Deborah, and others. De la tierra al cosmos: astronomía para niños [From the Earth to the Cosmos: Astronomy for Children]. 50p. Illustrated by Diego Echegaray and Juan González de León. ISBN 968-494-008-4.

595.78

Ortiz Monasterio P., Fernando, and Valentina Ortiz Monasterio
Garza. Mariposa Monarca vuelo de papel [Monarch Butter-
fly: Paper Flight]. 62p. Illustrated by José Luis
Alvarez. ISBN 968-494-009-2.

Ea. vol.: (La Brújula). México: Cidcli, 1984. $6.95. Gr. 6-9.

Spectacular photographs in color and simple illustrations about the universe and the Monarch butterfly are the best aspects of this scientific series. The purpose of De la tierra al cosmos: astronomía para niños is to show young readers fundamental aspects of the science of astronomy. It includes brief chapters on man and the sky, the solar system, spectacular phenomenons, the universe, the stars, and instruments to observe the sky. Mariposa Monarca, vuelo de papel relates various aspects about the Monarch butterfly, which is of Mexican origin. It tells about the migration, structure, life cycle, and need to protect it. Unfortunately, the author included a few unnecessary and disturbing notes in this otherwise fine introduction to the Monarch butterfly: His ten-year-old daughter's "stories" about the Monarch interspersed in the text as well as his incessant admonitions to young readers to protect nature.

CLASICOS INFANTILES ILUSTRADOS PROMEXA

Fiction

Andersen, Hans Christian. Almendrita [Thumbelina]. Illustrated by Susan Jeffers. Translated by José Emilio Pacheco. ISBN 968-34-0173-2.

_____. Los cisnes salvajes [The Wild Swans]. Illustrated by Susan Jeffers. Translated by José Emilio Pacheco. ISBN 968-34-0168-2.

Carroll, Lewis. "Alicia" para los niños [The Nursery Alice]. Illustrated by Tenniel. Translated by José Emilio Pacheco. ISBN 968-34-0185-6.

Lindgren, Astrid. El Tomten [Tomten]. Illustrated by Harald Wiberg. Translated by Yolanda Morena Rivas. ISBN 968-34-0177-5.

398.2

Basile, Giambattista. Petrosinella [Petrosinella]. Illustrated by Diane Stanley. Translated by Felipe Garrido. ISBN 968-34-0178-3.

Garrido, Felipe. Tajín y los siete truenos [Tajín and the Seven Thunderbolts]. Illustrated by Pedro Bayona. ISBN 968-34-0170-8.

Goble, Paul. El don del perro sagrado [The Gift of the Sacred Dog]. Illustrated by the author. Translated by Felipe Garrido. ISBN 968-34-0166-X.

Grimm, Jacob. La bella durmiente [Thorn Rose--Sleeping Beauty]. Illustrated by Errol le Cain. Translated by José Emilio Pacheco. ISBN 968-34-0164-3.

Jones, Harold. Fábulas de Esopo [Tales from Aesop]. Illustrated by the author. Translated by José Emilio Pacheco. ISBN 968-34-0179-1.

La Fontaine, Jean de. La tortuga y los dos patos [The Turtle and the Two Ducks]. Illustrated by Anne Rockwell. Translated by Ana Luz Trejo Lerdo. ISBN 968-34-0181-3.

Lang, Andrew. Aladino y la lámpara maravillosa [Aladdin and the Wonderful Lamp]. Illustrated by Errol Le Cain. Translated by José Emilio Pacheco. ISBN 968-34-0182-1.

Papp Severo, Emöke de. El bondadoso hermano menor [The Kindly Younger Brother]. Illustrated by Diane Goode. Translated by Felipe Garrido. ISBN 968-34-0174-0.

Perrault, Charles. La cenicienta o el zapatito de cristal [Cinderella or the Little Glass Slipper]. Illustrated by Errol Le Cain. Translated by José Emilio Pacheco. ISBN 968-34-0184-8.

Pushkin, Alexander. El cuento del gallo de oro [The Tale of the Golden Rooster]. Illustrated by I. Bilibin. Translated by José Emilio Pacheco. ISBN 968-34-0175-9.

_____. El cuento del zar Saltán o el príncipe y la princesa-cisne. [The Tale of the Czar Saltán or the Swan-Prince and Swan-Princess]. Illustrated by I. Bilibin. Translated by José Emilio Pacheco. ISBN 968-34-0169-4.

Ea. vol.: [40p.] (Clásicos Infantiles Ilustrados Promexa). México: Promexa, 1982. $5. Gr. 4-8.

Delightful selection of well-known fairy tales, legends, and fables from Denmark, Italy, Great Britain, Mexico, United States, Germany, France, Sweden, Hungary, and Russia are included in this outstanding series. These well-written Spanish versions make this series especially appealing to Spanish-speaking children who, up to now, lacked easy-to-read versions of the world's best loved stories. The gorgeous colorful illustrations and the attractive presentation of these books make them a treasure to own, to read, or to listen to.

COLECCION EL ZOO DE LOS BIBS

636.8

Prim, Victor, and Helena Rosa. La Gertrudis tiene gatitos [Gertrudis Has Kittens]. ISBN 84-344-0227-0.

636.6

_____, and _____. El loro busca casa [The Parrot Seeks a Home]. ISBN 84-344-0192-4.

636.7

_____, and _____. El perrito va a la escuela [The Puppy Goes to School]. ISBN 84-344-0194-0.

Ea. vol.: [20p.] (Colección El Zoo de los Bibs). Barcelona: Editorial Ariel, 1984. $6. Gr. 1-3.
Pablo and Julia Bibs, two happy middle-class Spanish children enjoy believable adventures with their new pets. The delightful, watercolor illustrations are refreshing and amusing. La Gertrudis tiene gatitos shows the Bibs family's adventures with newborn kittens. El loro busca casa tells about the parrot's search for a new home--a big tree in the family's patio. El perrito va a la escuela shows the family's experiences with their new puppy. Two pages at the end of each story describe basic facts about the care and feeding of these pets. Other titles in this series are El mono se disfraza [The Monkey Wears a Costume] and La tortuga vuelve a casa [The Turtle Returns Home].

COLECCION ELECTRONICA

794.8

Graham, Ian. Juegos de computadoras [Computer Games].
ISBN 84-7374-108-0.

789.9

Bingham, Ken. Manual de grabación: cassettes [Recording
Manual: Cassettes]. ISBN 84-7374-110-2.

005.1

Smith, Brian Reffin. Programación de computadoras [Com-
puter Programming]. ISBN 84-7374-109-9.

Ea. vol.: 48p. (Colección Electrónica). Madrid: Ediciones Plesa, 1983. $3.95. Gr. 5-10.
A great number of colorful illustrations and easy-to-
read explanations are the special characteristics of this
Eletronic Series in paperback, which also includes Calcula-
doras de bolsillo [Pocket Calculators] and Micro Computadoras [Microcomputers]. Juegos de computadoras describes popular computer and TV games and gives suggestions for winning at these games. Manual de grabación
includes descriptions of various cassette recorders and
gives numerous suggestions for making recordings. Programación de computadoras shows the functioning of a
computer and explains how to write programs in Basic.
These noteworthy publications begin by explaining elementary concepts and gradually allow the readers to complete fun projects with computers or tape recorders. Originally published in Great Britain.

COLECCION PIÑATA

574.5

Cárdenas, Magolo. La zona del silencio [The Silent Zone].
Illustrated by the author. ISBN 968-39-0077-1.

398

Ramírez, Elisa. Adivinanzas indígenas [Indigenous Riddles].
Illustrated by Máximino Javier. ISBN 968-39-0089-5.

Ea. vol.: 31p. (Colección Piñata). México: Editorial
Patria, 1984. $3. Gr. 1-3.
Like previous titles in this series, young children will
delight in the colorful illustrations and simple texts. La
zona del silencio narrates in a rhymed, easy-to-read text
a trip through a desert zone in northern Mexico. Adivinanzas indígenas is a collection of 12 riddles from ancient Mexico. The riddle is on one page, and the illustration on the
following page provides the answer. These books are indeed a charming introduction to Mexico.

COLECCION PIÑATA: LAS MATERIAS PRIMAS

677

Corona, Pascuala. La seda [Silk]. Illustrated by the author.
ISBN 968-39-0074-7.

633.6

Giron, Nicole. El azúcar [Sugar]. Illustrated by Ana Villa-
señor. ISBN 968-39-0099-2.

746.6

María, Beatriz de, and Campos Castelló. Tres colorantes pre-
hispánicos [Three Prehispanic Dyes]. Illustrated by Pascuala Corona. ISBN 968-39-0100-X.

676

Molina, Silvia. El papel [Paper]. Illustrated by Felipe Ugalde.
ISBN 968-39-0081-X.

Ea. vol.: 31p. (Colección Piñata: Las Materias Primas).
México: Editorial Patria, 1985. $3. Gr. 3-5.
Like previous titles in this series, these books introduce
children to the manual preparation of various products.
Colorful illustrations and simple, direct texts tell about the

94   Basic Collection of Books in Spanish

origin and production of silk in China and other countries,
about the growing and harvesting of sugar in rural Mexico, about the history and the cultivation of three pre-
Hispanic dyes in the state of Oaxaca in Mexico, and about
the manual preparation of paper as used in rural Mexico.

COLECCION ORBITA

551.6

Ford, Adam. Observando el clima [Observing the Climate].
ISBN 84-241-5704-4.

551

Lambert, David. Actividad de la tierra [Earth's Activities].
ISBN 84-241-5706-0.

621

Satchwell, John. Como funciona la energía [How Energy Func-
tions]. ISBN 84-241-5705-2.

Ea. vol.: 41p. Color photographs and drawings.
(Colección Orbita). Madrid: Editorial Everest, 1982. $5.
Gr. 6-9.
A straightforward text and attractive, colorful illustrations introduce young readers to the weather, the Earth in
motion, and various forms of energy. Each book is arranged in brief chapters with appropriate illustrations.
Some include simple, practical experiments. Because these
books were published in Europe, they use the metric system of measurement.

CUENTOS DE SIEMPRE

808.83

Cuentos de Andersen [Andersen's Stories]. Vol. 1. ISBN
84-7281-152-4.

398.2

Cuentos de Grimm [Grimm's Stories]. #8. ISBN 84-7281-152-4.

Ea. vol.: 16p. (Cuentos de Siempre). Madrid: Ediciones Auriga, 1984. $2.95. Gr. 5-8.

Delightful pastel illustrations and a fast-moving text re-
count the excitement of the original stories by Andersen
and Grimm: Cuentos de Andersen includes "El patito feo"
["The Ugly Duckling"], "El mechero" ["The Tinderbox"],
"Los cisnes slavajes" ["The Wild Swans"], and "La pequeña
vendedora de cerillas" ["The Little Match Girl"]. Cuentos
de Grimm includes "Los músicos de la ciudad de Bremen"
["The Bremen Town Musicians"], "Historia del hombre que
no tenía miedo" ["The Man of Iron"], and "El pescador y
su mujer" ["The Fisherman and His Wife"]. Other titles in
this series are Cuentos de Perrault, four different paperback publications; Cuentos de Andersen, two in addition
to the one reviewed; Cuentos de Grimm, two in addition to
the one reviewed.

EL HOMBRE Y LA NATURALEZA

551.5

Denou, Violeta. La fuerza de la naturaleza [Nature's Face].
ISBN 84-7183-133-3.

551.4

_____. El mar [The Sea]. ISBN 84-7183-164-3.

553

_____. La tierra y sus riquezas [The Earth's Riches].
ISBN 84-7183-193-7.

Ea. vol.: [26p.] Illustrated by the author. (El Hombre y la Naturaleza). Barcelona: Ediciones Hymsa, 1980.
$3. Gr. 4-7.

This series shows how people discover and use nature's
resources. Each book includes lively, witty illustrations
and a brief, direct text. La fuerza de la naturaleza discusses some of nature's forces and how we use them in our
lives and development. El mar describes the infinite riches
of the ocean. La tierra y sus riquezas introduces some of
Earth's riches, such as petroleum, gold, clay, phosphate,
and marble. These books are a joyful introduction to nature's resources.

EL HOMBRE Y SU ENTORNO

630

La agricultura [Agriculture].

582.16

Los árboles [Trees].

530

La física [Physics].

930.1

La arqueología [Archaeology].

549

Los minerales [Minerals].

598

Las aves [Birds].

560

Los animales prehistóricos [Prehistoric Animals].

738

La cerámica [Ceramics].

380.5

El transporte [Transportation].

612

El cuerpo humano [The Human Body].

728

La vivienda [Housing].

Ea. vol.: 52p. (El Hombre y su Entorno). Barcelona:
Afha Internacional, 1979. ISBN 84-201-0188-5 (for the
series). $6. Gr. 5-8.

As a basic introduction to humankind and the environment, this series does an adequate job. Each book has a
simple, direct text which gives basic information about
each topic supplemented with drawings in color that are a
bit stylized, thus detracting from their informational value.
The writing style and the drawings in this series, however,
will appeal to hitherto uninterested readers in these fields.

EL LIBRO DE...

551.4

Mayoral, María Teresa. El libro del agua y la vida [Book of
Water and Life]. Illustrated by Matías Rivera. 69p. ISBN
84-391-2009-5.

641.1

Sabugo Pintor, Angel. El libro de la alimentación [Book of
Nutrition]. Illustrated by Constantino Gatagan. 77p.
ISBN 84-391-2008-7.

574.5

_____. El libro del medio ambiente [Book of the Environ-
ment]. Illustrated by Constantino Gatagan. 76p. ISBN
84-391-2005-2.

Ea. vol.: León: Editorial Nebrija, 1980. $7.50. Gr.
6-9.

Basic facts about water, nutrition, and the environment are presented in each one of these books. A direct,
well-written text and a good selection of charts, maps,
drawings, and photographs (most in color) add to the
understanding of each topic. Each book ends with present
day problems and how they relate to the topic discussed.

EL MUSEO DE LOS DESCUBRIMIENTOS

520

Osman, Tony. El descubrimiento del universo [Discovery of the Universe]. ISBN 84-7374-048-3.

629.2

Summer, Philip, and Jenny Tyler. El nacimiento del automóvil [Birth of an Automobile]. ISBN 84-7374-029-7.

Ea. vol.: 48p. (El Museo de los Descubrimientos). Madrid: Ediciones Plesa, 1977. $6. Gr. 6-10.

A multitude of excellent drawings, maps, charts, and photographs and a well-written text are the salient characteristics of this series, which also includes titles on Africa, America, and money. El descubrimiento del universo discusses how humans have tried to study the skies since the Stone Age until modern-day space explorations. El nacimiento del automóvil begins with a description of transportation before automobiles and emphasizes the characteristics of the first automobiles and how they worked. Each book contains good explanations of technical information for the novice as well as the expert-to-be.

LOS NIÑOS Y LOS ANIMALES

949.4

Bonnardel, Rene. Lionel y los animales de la montaña [Lionel and the Mountain Animals]. ISBN 84-243-1392-5.

964

Tondeur, Freddy. Slimane y los animales del desierto [Slimane and the Desert Animals]. ISBN 84-243-1388-7.

Ea. vol.: 28p. Color photographs. (Los Niños y los Animales). Bilbao: Editorial Fher, 1980. $4.50. Gr. 5-8.

Outstanding color photographs of Lionel in the mountains of Switzerland and of Slimane in the Sahara Desert are the backgrounds of each of these books about boys in their

native regions and the various animals who also live there.
Each story relates the life of each boy, the animals that
thrive in the region, and the activities in which the boys
participate for recreation as well as survival. These books
are sure to please children seeking a fun story about animals or about life in other parts of the world.

OJOS ABIERTOS

307.7

Solano Flores, Guillermo. La calle [The Street]. Illustrated
by Gloria Calderas Lim. ISBN 968-24-1780-5.

_____. El campo [The Countryside]. Illustrated by Silvia
Luz Alvarado. ISBN 968-24-1779-1.

551.57

_____. La lluvia [The Rain]. Illustrated by Silvia Luz
Alvarado. ISBN 968-24-1778-3.

658.5

_____. El mercado [The Market]. Illustrated by Gloria
Calderas Lim. ISBN 968-24-1777-5.

529

_____. La noche [The Night]. Illustrated by Silvia Luz
Alvarado. ISBN 968-24-1781-3.

551.5

_____. El viento [The Wind]. Illustrated by Norma Jose-
fina Patiño Domínguez. ISBN 968-24-1871-2.

    Ea. vol.: 16p. (Ojos Abiertos). México: Editorial
Trillas, 1986. $3. Gr. 2-4.
    Young children are introduced to simple concepts through
unassuming illustrations in color and easy-to-read texts.
La calle describes various activities that take place on city
streets. El campo tells about life in the country among trees
and animals. La lluvia shows what happens when it rains.

El mercado shows a boy going to a market with his mother. La noche tells about nighttime activities. El viento describes what happens when there is a lot of wind. Other titles to be included in this series are: El periódico [The Newspaper], Mi propio museo [My Own Museum], El teatro [The Theater].

SERIE GERMAN Y ANA

551.4

Grée, Alain. El agua [Water]. ISBN 84-261-1706-6.

625.1

_____. El metro [The Subway]. ISBN 84-261-1853-4.

Ea. vol.: 29p. (Serie Germán y Ana). Barcelona: Editorial Juventud, 1981. $3. Gr. 4-6.

These books are the newest in a series whose purpose is to introduce children to various topics about nature and technology. Each book contains attractive color photographs and drawings of two children, Germán and Ana, as they learn about water and subways. These books are definitely excellent choices for children to learn about water and its uses and about the construction, use, and purposes of subways in large cities around the world.

Aboites, Luis. El campo y la ciudad [The Country and the
City]. Illustrated by Elena Climent. México: Editorial
Patria, 1983. 30p. ISBN 968-39-0059-3. $3. Gr. 2-4.
  Lucía, a girl who lives in the city, invites her cousin
Pedro, who lives in the country, to visit her for a few
days. Pedro does not like life in the city: He compares
the problems of city life to his peaceful life in the coun-
try. Adequate illustrations complement the simple text.

Aguirre Bellver, Joaquín. El juglar del Cid [Cid's Minstrel].
Madrid: Doncel, 1970. 135p. ISBN 84-325-0189-1. $13.
Gr. 3-8.
  This is a fascinating description of life in Spain during
the Middle Ages. It includes El Cid's exile, the Jews, the
life of a minstrel and a troubadour, and an outstanding
portrayal of the feelings and sufferings of an adolescent
boy.

Alcántara Sgarb, Ricardo. La bruja que quiso matar el sol
[The Witch Who Wanted to Kill the Sun]. Illustrated by
María Rius. Barcelona: Ediciones Hymsa, 1981? 32p.
ISBN 84-718-3183-X. $5. Gr. 3-6.
  Afkitán was an evil witch who didn't have any friends.
She wanted to hurt everyone, but what she hated the most
were the sun and water. The animals of the forest got
together to fight Afkitán. They selected a humble goose
to save the sun and water and frighten the terrible witch.
Exquisite animal illustrations and a lively text make this
story delightful reading.

101

102 Basic Collection of Books in Spanish

Almean, Fernando. Un solo de clarinete [A Clarinet Solo].
Illustrated by Margarita Puncel. Madrid: Ediciones S.M.,
1984. 107p. ISBN 94-348-1309-2. $7. Gr. 5-8.
   Ramón was not excited about spending his summer vacations in a small village in Spain. Even though he was
going to live with his grandparents, he did not know how
much fun children can have sliding in a granary, hiking
on a country road, going to old movie houses, watching
grandmother win a motorcycle race, and other extraordinary
activities. A few unaffected black-and-white illustrations
add a warm touch to the lighthearted text.

Alvarez, Agustín S. Aventuras de loberos [Adventures of
Wolf Hunters]. Adapted by Erna Wolf. Illustrated by
Luis Scafati. Buenos Aires: Aique Grupo Editor, S.R.L.,
1981. 47p. ISBN Unavailable. $5. Gr. 6-12.
   The adventures of a young student who joins a group
of gold prospectors in the southernmost part of Argentina
are full of excitement and action. The well-drawn characters, exotic setting, and fast tempo of the adaptation will
amaze and delight young readers. Striking and black and
white illustrations complement the story.

Amo, Montserrat del. Aparecen los "Blok" [The "Bloks" Ap-
pear]. Illustrated by Rita Culla. Barcelona: Juventud,
1971. 110p. ISBN 84-261-1043-6. $11. Gr. 3-6.
   Zestful, humorous adventures in the lives of Spanish
children describe their relationships with their parents,
their friends, and their pets. Life in a Spanish suburb
is delightfully explored.

Amo, Montserrat del. Zuecos y naranjas [Wooden Shoes and
Oranges]. Illustrated by Asun Balzola. Barcelona: La
Galera, 1981. 54p. ISBN 84-246-5505-2. $7. Gr. 4-8.
   Vicente, a young Spanish boy, attends a new school in
Denmark. There he meets Danish boys and girls who speak
a language that he cannot understand. Knud, a Danish
boy, is engrossed in drawing Vikings and wishes to teach
Vicente how to draw Vikings, but Vicente wants to draw a
bullfight--not Vikings. The two boys become good friends
when Vicente gives Knud an orange for dessert. (Fresh
oranges are special treats in Denmark.) Later Knud notices

that Vicente loves his "zuecos" (wooden shoes worn in Denmark) and gives him one in school and takes the other one
to his home after school. Vicente's oranges are an instant
success with all his classmates, even though Vicente's father misunderstood the nature of his "business."

Andersen, Hans Christian. Almendrita [Thumbelina]. Illustrated by Susan Jeffers. Translated by José Emilio Pacheco. México: Promexa, 1982. 40p. ISBN 968-34-0186-2.
   $5. Gr. 4-8.
   For full entry see series title, Clásicos Infantiles Ilustrados Promexa, in Section III.

Andersen, Hans Christian. Los cisnes salvajes [Wild Swans].
   Illustrated by Susan Jeffers. Translated by José Emilio
   Pacheco. México: Promexa, 1982. 40p. ISBN 968-34-
   0186-2. $5. Gr. 4-8.
   For full entry see series title, Clásicos Infantiles Ilus-
trados Promexa, in Section III.

Andersen, Hans Christian. El patito feo [The Ugly Duckling].
   Narrated by Marie Opperman. Illustrated by Johannes
   Larsen. Spanish version by Felipe Garrido. México:
   Promociones Editoriales Mexicanas, 1982. 50p. ISBN 968-
   34-0183-X. $5. Gr. 5-7.
   Good translation of The Ugly Duckling with colorful il-
lustrations.

Armijo, Consuelo. El mono imitamonos [A Monkey That Imi-
   tates Monkeys]. Illustrated by Alfonso Ruano. Madrid:
   Ediciones S.M., 1984. 60p. ISBN 84-348-1285-1. $7.
   Gr. 3-5.
   A young, happy monkey loved to play on the trees
close to his mother. One day he got lost and, unknowing-
ly, arrived in the city. There he scared a businessman,
entertained an old lady, and befriended Tere and Papito,
a brother and sister, who took him to their house where
he amused the whole family with his monkey-like behavior.
Finally, his mother found him and took him home again.
   The simple, two-tone illustrations are a good complement
to the amusing, lighthearted text.

Armijo, Consuelo. El Pampinoplas [The Pampinoplas]. Illustrated by Antonio Tello. Madrid: Ediciones, S.M., 1980.
100p. ISBN 84-348-0828-5. $5. Gr. 4-8.

Poliche, who is approximately 12 years old, spends an
unforgettable summer vacation with his grandfather in the
country. They get involved in innumerable adventures,
such as building a homemade bicycle, exploring dangerous
territory, persecuting the town's thief, organizing a party
for grandfather's childhood friends, and other exciting and
fun activities. Unfortunately, there are only eight black-
and-white illustrations; but the simple, light-hearted text
is indeed a joy to read.

Ballesta, Juan. Tommy y el elefante [Tommy and the Elephant].
Barcelona: Editorial Lumen, 1983. [26p.] ISBN 84-3578-5.
$3. Gr. 3-5.

Tommy, a little boy, had a close friend--an imaginary
elephant named Pac. Pac accompanied Tommy wherever he
went. He also protected Tommy from unforeseen dangers
and difficult adults. Everything was fine until Tommy's
aunt suggested that he visit a psychoanalyst. Tommy's
logic and the amusing illustrations should appeal to sophis-
ticated children.

Belgrano, Margarita. Los zapatos voladores [The Flying Shoes].
Illustrated by Chacha. Buenos Aires: Centro Editor de
América Latina, 1978. 26p. ISBN Unavailable. $7. Gr.
2-4.

A few people in town saw the "flying shoes." The next
day the news was all over town and nobody went to work;
everybody wanted to see the "flying shoe" that was trapped
on top of the TV antenna of the pharmacist's house. The
governor pleaded with the people to go back to work and
to ignore the story of the "flying shoes." Meanwhile, firemen presented him with the "flying shoe," but the governor
insisted that it was only a shoe. Amidst this commotion,
there appeared a barefooted mailman who explained that he
had thrown his shoes out of the window because he got
tired of walking and couldn't afford a bicycle. So everybody contributed towards the mailman's new shoes and bicycle.

The amusing illustrations and light-hearted text will
please young readers.

Bergström, Gunilla. ¡Que duermas bien Alfonso! [Sleep Well,
   Alfonso!]. Translated by Ana Valdés. Stockholm: Editorial Nordan, 1984. [24p.] ISBN 91-7702-083-9. Gr. 3-5.
      Alfonso, a four-year-old boy, does not want to go to
   sleep even though it is past his bedtime. His kind and
   understanding father does everything he can to help Alfonso go to sleep. He reads him a story, brings him his
   toothbrush, brings him a glass of water, brings him a
   chamber pot, looks for a hidden lion in the closet, and
   searches everywhere for Alfonso's teddy bear. After all
   of his activity, Alfonso's father falls asleep in the middle
   of the living room floor. As there is no one else to cater
   to Alfonso's demands, little Alfonso goes to sleep too. The
   modernistic illustrations perfectly complement this story
   about a little boy and his devoted father. (Interestingly,
   there is no mention of a mother at home.)

Bergström, Gunilla. ¿Quién te asuuusta Alfonso? [Who Scaaares
   You, Alfonso?]. Translated by Ana Luisa Valdes. Stockholm: Editorial Nordan, 1983. 28p. ISBN 91-7702-079-0.
   $6. Gr. 3-5.
      Alfonso, a little boy, deals with his own fears about
   ghosts. At times he tells himself that they don't really
   exist. But when he is alone at night his fears become
   much stronger. His father tries to help him overcome his
   fear of ghosts by teaching him a song that he should sing
   calmly and clearly every time he thinks about ghosts.
   Modernistic illustrations of a little boy and his father add
   a humorous touch to this story about a boy's true feelings.

Blume, Judy. La ballena [Blubber]. Translated by Alma
   Flor Ada. Scarsdale, N.Y.: Bradbury Press, dist. by
   Macmillan, 1983. 172p. ISBN 0-02-710940-2. $5. Gr. 5-
   7.
      Jill, a thin fifth-grader, joins the rest of her class in
   tormenting Linda, an overweight girl. Later, she finds
   out that she, too, will become the target of much scorn
   and abuse by the other children. Well-done translation of
   Blubber.

Blume, Judy. ¿Estás ahí Dios? Soy yo, Margaret [Are You
   There God? It's Me, Margaret]. Translated by Alma Flor

Ada. Scarsdale, N.Y.: Bradbury Press, 1983. 159p.
ISBN 0-02-710950-X. $9.95. Gr. 4-6.

Margaret, a 12-year-old, is faced with the problems of growing up: choosing a religion, wearing a bra, menstruation, and normal family arguments. This is a good translation of Are You There God? It's Me, Margaret, with a few typos that do not detract from the lively and amusing story of a girl and her private dialogues with her God.

Burningham, John. Harquin el zorro que bajó al valle [Harquin, The Fox Who Went Down to the Valley]. Illustrated by the author. Valladolid: Editorial Miñón, 1975. 30p. ISBN 84-355-0437-9. $9. Gr. 3-5.

Harquin is a young fox who ventured down to the valley in spite of his parent's repeated warnings. One day the forest ranger saw him and told the leader of the fox hunt about the foxes. Thus, Harquin had to act fast to avoid having all his family shot by the fox hunters. Striking illustrations complement this amusing story, originally published in England in 1967.

Cabré, Jaume. El extraño viaje que nadie se creyó (La historia que Roc Pons no conocía). [The Strange Journey No One Believed (The Story Roc Pons Did Not Know)]. Illustrated by Joan Andreu Vallvé. Barcelona: La Galera, 1980. 118p. ISBN 84-246-4541-3. $8. Gr. 6-10.

Roc Pons, a 14-year-old boy from Barcelona, found himself in a strange century. He left his house one summer afternoon in 1980, and suddenly realized he was in Barcelona in 1714--the year the city was blockaded by Castilian and French armies which supported Phillip V. Black-and-white line illustrations and a fast-paced text convey to readers the feelings of the people of Barcelona that preceded the surrender of their city. Roc's adventures and dilemmas add much interest and excitement to this story, which was written by the author as a homage to his city, Barcelona, in its fight for freedom.

Calders, Pere. Cepillo [Brush]. Illustrated by Carme Solé Vendrell. Barcelona: Ediciones Hymsa, 1981. 24p. ISBN 87-718-3181-3. $3. Gr. 3-5.

When a young boy realized that his mother was going to

give the family's dog away because it had eaten his father's
hat, he searched for a new companion. Finally in the at-
tic he found an old brush. He tied a rope to the brush
and thus pretended that he owned a strange dog. "Brush"
followed him everywhere, and at night he noticed that
"Brush" moved like a dog. His mother and father wouldn't
believe him, until one night when a thief came into the
house, and "Brush" ran to save his father. So, "it is not
sure that it is, but he may very well be."

Attractive, colorful illustrations complement this touching story about a boy and his "dog."

Carroll, Lewis. "Alicia" para los niños [The Nursery Alice].
Illustrated by Tenniel. Translated by José Emilio Pacheco.
México: Promexa, 1982. 40p. ISBN 968-34-0185-6. $5.
Gr. 4-8.

For full entry see series title, Clásicos Infantiles Ilustrados Promexa, in Section III.

Carruth, Jane. El diente molesto [The Annoying Tooth].
Illustrated by Tony Hutchings. Translated by Liliana Rey.
Buenos Aires: Editorial Sigmar, 1982. 20p. ISBN 950-
11-0191-6. $3. Gr. 3-5.

Nucho, a squirrel, loves to eat candy and forgets to
brush his teeth. When his tooth starts to hurt, he is ter-
rified about going to the dentist. Finally, his mother
takes him to the dentist and Nucho never again forgets to
brush his teeth. As a reminder to children, this book may
serve a useful purpose.

Claret, María. La ratita Blasa [Blasa, the Mouse]. Barcelona:
Editorial Juventud, 1983. 28p. ISBN 84-261-1957-3. $5.
Gr. 3-5.

Blasa is a pretty little rat. She lived alone, but one
day decided to get married. She met a duck, but he loved
to swim in cold water. She met a sparrow, but he loved
to fly all the time. She met a lamb, but he loved to jump.
She met a frog, but he loved to stay in the water. And
so on, until one day she met a little gray rat.... Charming, pastel illustrations show Blasa with her many suitors.

Cleary, Beverly. Henry Huggins. Illustrated by Louis Dar-
    ling. Translated by Argentina Palacios. New York: Wil-
    liam Morrow and Co., 1983. 159p. ISBN 0-688-02014-3.
    $10.25. Gr. 4-6.
        The popular adventures of Henry Huggins and his be-
    loved dog, Ribsy, are now available for Spanish readers
    in this well-done translation that has maintained the flavor
    and fun of the original. Spanish translations of famous
    American books are always in demand by eager Spanish
    readers; this one will be no exception.

Cleary, Beverly. Ramona la chinche [Ramona the Pest].
    Illustrated by Louis Darling. Translated by Argentina
    Palacios. New York: William Morrow and Co., 1984. 181p.
    ISBN 0-688-02783-0. $9.50. Gr. 4-6.
        The delightfully human experiences of Ramona Quimby
    in kindergarten class are now available for Spanish-speaking
    readers. Ramona's sad and happy times as well as her
    many misunderstandings with her parents, teacher and
    friends have been well translated into an easy-flowing Span-
    ish. It must be noted that the translator has done an es-
    pecially fine job of describing incidents which have special
    meaning to English-speaking children in the U.S., such as
    Halloween parties in school and Ramona's confusion regard-
    ing "The Star Spangled B-banner" (p. 163), which other-
    wise could not have been understood by Spanish-speaking
    children unfamiliar with customs in the U.S.

Company, Mercè. La casa del Gatus [Gatus' House]. Illus-
    trated by Montserrat Ginesta. Translated by Angelina
    Gatell. Barcelona: La Galera, S.A. Editorial, 1984. 54p.
    ISBN 84-246-3815-8. $4.50. Gr. 4-7.
        Nobody knew the real name of the short, eccentric,
    smiling, old man, who everybody in town called Gatus. He
    lived alone in a very strange place--under a bridge close
    to town. Suddenly, an old woman and an old man who
    also did not have a home of their own, asked Gatus if they
    could share a piece of the bridge. The three old people
    worked together to help each other and make a living. The
    people in town decided to help them, first by giving them
    odd jobs, and then by fixing up an old house for them.
    But, a terrible storm took the old people away before they
    could move to their new home. Two-tone, realistic illustra-

tions add a touching glow to this heart-warming story
about delightful, old people.

Company, Mercè. ¿Dónde está el tío Ramón? [Where is Uncle
Ramón?]. Illustrated by Agustí Asensio. Barcelona:
Editorial Timun Mas, S.A., 1982. 36p. ISBN 84-7176-
499-7. $7. Gr. 4-7.
Pedro, Victor, and their cousin Elia were prepared to
spend their holidays with Uncle Ramón in his home by the
sea. When Uncle Ramón did not meet them at the railroad
station, the cousins started on a hike which led them to a
deserted castle, two bandits, and an imprisoned Uncle
Ramón. Through young Victor's daring actions, the whole
group is saved, the bandits are captured, and the cousins
are ready to begin their vacations. Even though one may
question the bandits' gullibility, this is a quick-paced story
with engaging characters and delightful, colorful illustrations.

Company, Mercè. Perdidos en la cueva [Lost in the Cave].
Illustrated by Agustí Asensio. Barcelona: Editorial Timun
Mas, 1983. 36p. ISBN 84-776-529-2. $9. Gr. 5-7.
The extraordinary adventures of two boys and a girl
who get lost inside a cave are narrated in a witty, fast-
paced style. Charming illustrations capture the suspense
of this story as the children try to find their way out of
what seems to be an enchanted cave.

Company, Mercè. El prisonero del gigante [The Giant's Pris-
oner]. Illustrated by Agustí Asensio. Barcelona: Hymsa,
1982. [26p.] ISBN 84-7.183-203-8. $6.50. Gr. 3-5.
Bernardo, the king's son, is captured by a lonely giant.
He elicits everybody's help to get out, but everything
fails. Finally, a big snow storm allows him to escape and
return home. Well-told story with attractive illustrations.

Cos, Rosa Ma. Historias fantásticas de Ivo y Tino: el bosque
encantado [Ivo and Tino's Fantastic Stories]. Barcelona:
Editorial Timun Mas, S.A., 1981? 26p. ISBN 84-7176-
301-9. $6. Gr. 3-5.
Through striking, colorful illustrations and two children,

Ivo and Tino, who set out on an imaginary excursion in an
enchanted forest, readers are exposed to the wonders of
nature: animals of the forest, the importance of water and
wind, precious jewels, and the beauty of flowers. This is
a delightful complement to the study of nature.

Counhaye, Guy. Victor, el hipopótamo volador [Victor, the
Flying Hippopotamus]. Illustrated by Marie-José Sacré.
León: Editorial Everest, 1982. 28p. ISBN 84-241-5309-X.
$6. Gr. 3-5.
    Victor, a hippopotamus, was born with wings. His
wings were not very large--they were the size of the wings
of a fly. At first, Victor was sad because he wasn't like
the others, but soon he saw the advantage of wings and
decided to see the world. Victor's adventures in the sky,
in the city, in the country, and finally in a circus where
he met Petunia, a pretty female hippopotamus who also had
wings like Victor, are told in a simple, direct style. Striking, watercolor illustrations of Victor in ludicrous situations
will amuse young readers.

D'Atri, Adriana. El amigo nuevo [The New Friend]. Illustrated by Ulises Wensell. Madrid: Ediciones Altea, 1981.
32p. ISBN 84-372-1580-3. $4. Gr. 2-4.
    Makoto, a seven-year-old boy from Japan, just moved
with his family to a new home in Spain. There he meets
his new neighbors who immediately invite him to play with
them. Makoto shows his new friends pictures of his old
home and tells them about the problems of moving to a new
country. Even though the problems of adjusting to a new
country and language may be too simplistic, the cultural
differences between Makoto and his new friends may be
understood by young readers.

D'Atri, Adriana. El premio [The Prize]. Illustrated by Ulises
Wensell. Madrid: Ediciones Altea, 1980. 32p. ISBN 84-
372-1487-4. $4. Gr. 2-4.
    Fernando won several prizes for his beautiful paintings.
Thus he invited all his friends to the zoo. There they
enjoy looking at many animals and feeding the ducks. They
also found out that Fernando's painting won the first prize.
Charming illustrations of natural-looking children dominate
each scene.

D'Atri, Adriana. El viejo teatro [The Old Theatre]. Illustrated by Ulises Wensell. Madrid: Ediciones Altea, 1981.
31p. ISBN 84-372-1482-3. $4. Gr. 2-4.

Gabriel invites his friends to an old downtown theatre.
At the end of the show, the boys and girls cannot find
Gabriel. Finally they find him in a secret room under the
theater stage. Through Gabriel's experiences, young readers are exposed to life inside a theater.

de Paola, Tomie. Oliver Button es un nena [Oliver Button Is
a Sissy]. Illustrated by the author. Translated by
Fernando Alonso. Valladolid: Editorial Miñón, S.A., 1982.
46p. ISBN 84-355-0631-2. $4. Gr. 3-5.

The touching story of Oliver Button, a boy who wanted
to pick flowers, jump rope, paint pictures, read books,
and dance, but did not want to play ball with the other
boys, is now available in Spanish. Boys and girls will
empathize with Oliver's attempt to win an artists' contest
through his dancing.

Delgado, Eduardo. Los Mecs cocineros [The Cooking Mecs].
Illustrated by Helena Rosa. Barcelona: Editorial Timun
Mas, 1982. [26p.] ISBN 84-7176-416-4. $3.50. Gr. 2-4.

Sergio, the chef, was worried because none of his help-
ers showed up for work. Thus, the Mecs, two boys and
two girls, volunteered to help. After much confusion and
a few broken dishes, the food was a success. Pastel illustrations of children at work in the kitchen complement
the easy-to-read text.

Delgado, Eduardo. Los Mecs juegan a ser actores [The Mecs
Pretend to Be Actors]. Illustrated by Helena Rosa. Barcelona: Editorial Timun Mas, 1980? [22p.] ISBN 84-7176-
404-0. $3.50. Gr. 3-5.

The Mecs, two boys and two girls, decide to produce a
play. They work on the scenery, musical accompaniment,
costumes, and make-up. The day of the performance they
make a few mistakes but everybody enjoys it. Pastel illustrations complement the simple text.

Delgado, Eduardo. Los Mecs juegan en la playa [The Mecs

Play at the Beach]. Illustrated by Helena Rosa. Barcelona: Editorial Timun Mas, 1982. [26p.] ISBN 84-7176-
417-2. $3.50. Gr. 2-4.
   The Mecs, two boys and two girls, spend a day at the
beach with their grandfather. Their activities include
cleaning up the beach, visiting the surrounding area, building a sand castle and looking at an endangered whale.
Pastel illustrations of happy children at the beach complement the easy-to-read text.

Delgado, Eduardo. Los Mecs van de excursión [The Mecs Go
   on an Excursion]. Illustrated by Helena Rosa. Barcelona:
   Editorial Timun Mas, 1981. [22p.] ISBN 84-7176-402-4.
   $3.50. Gr. 3-5.
   The Mecs, two boys and two girls, and grandfather
Pablo go on an excursion to collect plants, animals, and
stones for a show in their neighborhood. Their trip to
the country is full of excitement and happy findings.
Pastel illustrations of busy children enliven the text.

Delgado, Eduardo. Los Mecs van en bicicleta [The Mecs on
   a Bicycle]. Illustrated by Helena Rosa. Barcelona: Editorial Timun Mas, 1980? [24p.] ISBN 84-7176-415-6.
   $3.50. Gr. 2-4.
   The Mecs, two boys and two girls, became interested
in bicycles after attending a bicycle competition. First,
they play at home with toy bicycles, then they decide to
build their own three-wheel bikes, and finally they play
games with two real bikes. Pastel illustrations of children
at play with their bicycles complement the easy-to-read
text. (One illustration of a boy without pants may be ob-
jectionable to some adults.)

Denou, Violeta. Nico y Ana pescadores [Nico and Ana Fisher-
   man]. Barcelona: Editorial Timun Mas, 1982? [28p.]
   ISBN 84-7176-432-6. $3. Gr. 2-4.
   Nico and Ana spend a few days with their cousins in
a Spanish fishing village. There they learn about the life
of fishermen, the sale of fish, fishing with nets and poles,
and fishing underwater. Vivacious illustrations of fishermen at work and at play enliven the easy-to-read text.

Durán, Carlos Joaquín. Viaje al planeta misterioso [Journey
to the Mystery Planet]. Buenos Aires: Aique Grupo Editor, 1980. 64p. ISBN Unavailable. $7. Gr. 5-8.
  This is a simply told science fiction story which includes a "good" robot, an inventor, his wife and two children, and a "bad" scientist. They live in the year 3125
in a city where there wasn't a single green tree or plant
left: "Todo había sido plastificado, pavimentado, desin-
fectado, aprovechado, techado y cerrado. [Everything had
been plastified, paved, disinfected, used, covered with a
roof, and closed.]" (p. 11).
  When the family goes on vacation to a mysterious planet,
they encounter serious danger as the bad scientist wishes
to kill them by changing the robot's signals. The contrast
of life in a highly developed planet and in a plant which
was full of "natural life" is a bit exaggerated, but the excitement of the story certainly maintains the reader's interest. Unoriginal textbook-like illustrations of outer space
complement the text.

Gantschev, Ivan. El lago de la luna [The Moon Lake]. Translated by Francisco Gonzáles Aramburo. México: Editorial
Trillas, 1985. [28p.] ISBN 968-24-1680-9. $3. Gr. 4-6.
  An old shepherd and his grandson, Pedro, lived alone
in the mountains. When the old shepherd died, Pedro con-
tinued happily caring for his sheep. One day one of his
sheep wandered off into a huge ravine and into moon lake
where Pedro found precious jewels and a wise fox, who
taught him an important secret about moon lake. Striking
watercolor illustrations add an appropriate mood to this
story about a courageous shepherd boy.

Graves, Robert. El gran libro verde [The Big Green Book].
Illustrated by Maurice Sendak. Translated by Lucia Graves.
Barcelona: Editorial Lumen, S.A., 1983. 63p. ISBN 84-
264-3580-7. $5. Gr. 3-5.
  The Big Green Book, originally published in the U.S.
in 1962, is now available for Spanish readers. Jack's mag-
ical adventures with his aunt, uncle, and a big dog that
ran after rabbits are complemented by Maurice Sendak's
witty black-and-white illustrations to the delight of all
readers.

Haugen, Tormond. Los pájaros de la noche [Birds of the Night]. Translated by Roser Berdagué. Barcelona: Editorial Juventud, 1984. 144p. ISBN 84-261-2056-3. $8. Gr. 6-10.

Jake's father was not like other fathers. He often refused to go to work. Also, he would disappear and not tell anybody where he was going. Jake's feelings of frustration, anxiety, and helplessness are very well depicted in this realistic novel about a boy who must cope with an unreliable father and a hard-working, but tired mother. Some adolescents may sympathize with the despair of a boy growing up in an unstable family with serious human problems, where there are no easy solutions nor, apparently, happy endings. This novel was originally published in 1973 in Norway and, subsequently, won a literary award for young adults in Germany.

Hemingway, Ernest. El buen león [The Good Lion]. Illustrated by Francisco J. González. Translated by Francisco Pabón Torres. Madrid: Editorial Debate, 1984. 37p. ISBN 84-7444-137-4. $5.95. Gr. 3-5.

A good lion, who was originally from Venice, Italy, spent a difficult time in Africa among "bad" lions who ate zebras, antelope, or other animals every day. The bad lions did not like him and made fun of the wings the good lion had on his back. One day the bad lions threatened to kill the good lion so he flew back home to Venice where he enjoyed life with his friends. Attractive watercolor illustrations add an amusing tone to this unusual story of "bad" and "good" lions.

Hemingway, Ernest. El toro fiel [The Faithful Bull]. Illustrated by Arcadio Lobato. Translated by Francisco Pabón Torres. Madrid: Editorial Debate, 1982. 35p. ISBN 84-7444-0666-1. $4.50. Gr. 2-4.

The delightful story about a faithful, brave bull who falls in love with a pretty cow and hence was sent to fight and die at a bullfight is very well translated into Spanish. Striking watercolor illustrations complement the easy-to-read text.

Heuer, Margarita. El conejo Carlitos [Carlitos the Rabbit].

Illustrated by Luis Ceballos. México: Editorial Trillas, 1983. [24p.] ISBN 968-24-1382-6. $3. Gr. 3-5.

Carlitos, a white rabbit, had a big problem: He did not know what animal he would like to be when he grew up. So, after thinking about it, he decided to become a lion. He tried his strength against an armadillo, who convinced him to look at himself in the lake. But it took a ferocious lion and a pretty female lion to make him wonder if "lions" would ever like carrots, cabbages, and pretty female rabbits. This is truly an entertaining story with cartoon-like illustrations.

Ichikawa, Satomi. Susana y Nicolás en el mercado [Susan and Nicholas at the Market]. Translated by Ramón Andrés González. Barcelona: Plaza y Janes, 1979. 29p. ISBN 84-01-70064-7. $4. Gr. 3-5.

Delightful pastel illustrations and a direct text tell about Susana and Nicolás' first trip to a rural open-air market. Their mother gave them a shopping list which included vegetables, fish, fruit, milk, a straw basket, yarn, flowers, and bread. The obvious intent of this story is to show children doing the shopping and thinking about the products they buy in a rural setting.

Jané, Jordi. Juanote y las tres bolsas de oro [Juanote and the Three Bags of Gold]. Illustrated by Joma. Translated by José A. Pastor Cañada. ISBN 84-246-1647-0.

Sennell, Joles. El mejor novio del mundo [The Best Suitor in the World]. Illustrated by Carme Peris. Translated by José A. Pastor Cañada. ISBN 84-246-1648-0.

Ea. vol.: [24p.] (Cuentos Populares). Barcelona: La Galera, 1984. $5. Gr. 3-6.

These are the two newest titles in this series of 47 popular stories with engaging texts and alluring watercolor illustrations. Juanote y las tres bolsas de oro shows how a poor boy became wealthy after visiting other lands and using common sense to solve other people's problems. El mejor novio del mundo tells how the papa and mama of the prettiest mouse in the world go in search of a suitor for their daughter. After exploring the situation with the sun,

a cloud, the wind, and the Chinese Wall, they decide that
the best suitor is their neighbor--a mouse who had been
in love with their daughter for a long time. The only re-
grettable aspect about these stories is the series of questions and review topics at the end of the stories. These
"exercises" are sure to detract from the stories' appeal
and enjoyment.

Kurtz, Carmen. Oscar y la extraña luz [Oscar and the
Strange Light]. Illustrated by Odile Kurz. Barcelona:
Editorial Juventud, 1984. 175p. ISBN 84-261-2045-8.
$6.50. Gr. 6-9.
    Oscar, a 12-year-old boy, and Rafael Roca, a wealthy
Spanish industrialist, are kidnapped by a gang of incom-
petent characters. In their escape, Oscar and Mr. Roca
are aided by a beautiful pregnant young woman, two young
women who excel in judo, an older, brave woman who did
not mind jumping out of windows, and other kind people
who went out of their way to make sure that the victims
return home safely. The greatest hero of them all is a
laser that is constantly on the lookout for Oscar and allows
him to perform incredible feats when all else seems to fail.
At the end, the kidnappers are forgiven and everybody
lived happily ever after. This is a fast-paced adventure
story with a few strange occurrences: A woman gives
birth assisted by the heroes, and the laser is never a
convincing force.

Kurtz, Carmen. Veva [Veva]. Illustrated by Odile Kurz.
Barcelona: Editorial Noguer, S.A., 1980. 118p. ISBN
84-279-3120-4. $6. Gr. 6-10.
    Veva is a nine-month-old baby girl who can talk and
think like an adult. She tells about life with her family,
and other amusing experiences that surround her life in
Spain. She begins by describing her birth, which "[was
something exclusively between my mother and me ... difficult, yes, but if others have done it ... why couldn't
I?]"; her first meal at her mother's breast; her wishes to
be loved by her family; her special relationship with a
gentle and understanding grandmother; and her impatience
with her 18-year-old sister, Natacha.
    Veva's family is real and thus charms us with all the
jealousy, pain, and joy that occur in a normal, busy family.

The witty dialogue and humorous situations will appeal to young readers who will enjoy reading about the life of a middle-class family in Spain.

Kurusa. La calle es libre [The Street Is Free]. Illustrated by Monika Doppert. Caracas: Ediciones Ekaré-Banco del Libro, 1981. [44p.] ISBN Unavailable. $4. Gr. 5-8.
   Realistic story and illustrations about life in the slums of Caracas, Venezuela that tells how a group of children, who did not have a place to play, organized the whole neighborhood, and constructed their own park on an empty lot. This story will have more meaning to Latin American children who can sympathize with the problems of police abuse and bureaucratic indifference.

Lindgren, Astrid. Madita [Madita]. Illustrated by Ilon Wikland. Translated by Herminia Dauer. Barcelona: Editorial Juventud, 1983. 192p. ISBN 84-261-1729-5. $6. Gr. 5-7.
   Madita, a seven-year-old girl, and her younger sister, Lisabet, live with their parents in a small town in Sweden. In typical Lindgren easy-going style, the reader is exposed to the girls' adventures at home, such as jumping from a roof using an umbrella as a parachute with dire results, at school with make-believe friends, and celebrating Christmas and Easter with neighbors and friends. The refreshing personalities of Madita and Lisabet, as well as the quick pace of their amusing adventures, will capture many girls' interests. I wonder, though, if girls who can read this story (fifth- to seventh-graders) will not find these adventures too childish. Small, black-and-white line illustrations of the two girls in various predicaments complement the story.

Lindgren, Astrid. El Tomten [Tomten]. Illustrated by Harald Wiberg. Translated by Yolanda Morena Rivas. México: Promexa, 1982. 40p. ISBN 968-34-0177-5. $5. Gr. 4-8.
   For full entry see series title, Clásicos Infantiles Ilustrados Promexa, in Section III.

Lindgren, Astrid. Yo también quiero tener hermanos [I, Too,

Want Brothers]. Illustrated by Ilon Wikland. Translated
by Herminia Dauer. Barcelona: Editorial Juventud, 1981.
32p. ISBN 84-261-1742-2. $4. Gr. 3-5.
  Pedro's feelings regarding his new baby sister, Elena,
are honestly depicted in this warm story with lovable illustrations. It includes a simple explanation of birth, as
well as an excellent portrayal of Pedro's anger and jealousy
because of his mother's constant attention to his new baby
sister.

Llimona, Mercedes. Bibí y el verano [Bibí and Summer]. Illustrated by the author. Barcelona: Ediciones Hymsa,
1982. 24p. ISBN 84-7.183-198-8. $7. Gr. 2-4.
  Bibí, a young girl, has many activities planned during
the summer: First, she and her two cousins are invited
to spend a few days in the country at their grandparents'
house. Upon her return, her parents take Bibí and her
friend Jorge to a beach resort. Lighthearted, pastel illustrations show Bibí and her family and friends enjoying
summer activities in Spain.

Llimona, Mercedes. Bibí y la primavera [Bibí and Spring].
Illustrated by the author. Barcelona: Ediciones Hymsa,
1981. 24p. ISBN 84-7183-170-8. $7. Gr. 2-4.
  Bibí, a little girl, and her neighbor Jorge realize that
spring is here. There are many things they enjoy doing:
riding a bike, helping mother clean house, painting a
mural at school, eating strawberry cake, and going on a
hike. Also, Bibí wins the gymnastics contest at school.
Attractive illustrations of children and springtime complement the story.

Lööf, Jan. Historia de una manzana roja [The Story of a Red
Apple]. Illustrated by the author. Valladolid: Editorial
Miñón, 1982. [28p.] ISBN 84-355-0417-4. $8. Gr. 2-4.
  What happens when a man who sells fresh fruit wants
to deceive an unsuspecting customer is wittingly told in
this story that neither of the two main characters can understand. Young readers will enjoy the fast action and
engaging illustrations. (This story was originally published
in Denmark in 1974.)

Molina Llorente, Pilar. El mensaje de maese Zamaor [Maese
  Zamaor's Message]. Illustrated by Francisco Sole. Madrid:
  Ediciones S.M., 1981. 107p. ISBN 84-348-0886-2. $9.
  Gr. 6-10.
      Maese Zamaor, court painter of Cártulo II, is selected
  by the King for a dangerous mission: He must deliver a
  secret document to the king's cousin, the Prince of Zar-
  duña, if the kingdom is to survive. Maese Zamaor experiences many hardships and humiliations as he confronts
  abusive landlords, thieves, and traitors, as well as suffer-
  ing hunger, cold, and lack of sleep. By using his talents
  as an artist, his intelligence, and his courage, Zamaor discovers the traitor and saves the kingdom of Cártulo II,
  King of Fartuel.
      The adventures and excitement of Maese Zamaor's diffi-
  cult journey are an engrossing story which will maintain
  the interest of young readers. Eight black-and-white line
  illustrations excellently depict the life of a brave Spanish
  artist and courier.

Olaizola, José Luis. Cucho [Cucho]. Illustrated by Antonio
  Tello. Madrid: Ediciones S.M., 1983. 96p. ISBN 84-
  348-1169-3. $6. Gr. 6-10.
      Cucho, a ten-year-old Spanish boy, did not have a
  father or a mother, but because other children did not
  have a grandmother, he felt they were equal. Thus begins this high-spirited story about Cucho and his grandmother who, despite their poverty, manage to make their
  life in Madrid a series of successful and vivacious experiences. The incidents portrayed in Cucho's life may seem
  far-fetched to young readers in many countries, but they
  are plausible, and what's more important, the author has
  conceived several refreshing and buoyant characters.

Otero, Rodolfo. Milla Loncó [Milla Loncó]. Buenos Aires:
  Editorial Acme, 1984. 207p. ISBN 950-565-222-4. $6.50.
  Gr. 6-10.
      This novel, which won the 1983 Robin Hood Award for
  adolescents, tells about life in the dangerous Argentinian
  frontier in the late 1800s. Two teen-age boys and an 18-
  year-old girl are kidnapped by the Indians. They suffer
  insults and abuse in the hands of their captors, but, ultimately, through their courage and perseverance, they

manage to escape. This is not an outstanding historical
novel, but rather a fast-paced story full of adventure and
excitement on almost every page. It will maintain the interest of young readers searching for adventure in the Argentinian plains.

Pacheco, M.A., and J.L. García Sánchez. El viaje de nunca
acabar [The Never Ending Journey]. Illustrated by Ulises
Wensell. Madrid: Ediciones Altea, 1976. 44p. ISBN 84-
372-1273-1. $5. Gr. 3-6.
    Witty story with attractive illustrations about Augusto
and his amazing trip on all kinds of transportation: bus,
ship, plane, donkey, camel, train, helicopter, pipeline,
and car. Finally he decides to mail the cheese to his Aunt
Leocadia, as Augusto is going again on another trip.

Patience, John. Las estaciones en Valdehelechos [The Seasons
in Valdehelechos]. Illustrated by the author. Translated
by Diorki. Madrid: Editorial Everest, 1982. 61p. ISBN
84-241-5270-0. $7. Gr. 2-4.
    The animals who live in Valdehelechos are good friends
and good neighbors. In this story, they relate their activities during spring, summer, fall, and winter in which
they enjoy nature, their families, and each other. Outstanding color illustrations are the main attraction of this
beautiful book.

Paz, Marcela. Papelucho [Papelucho]. Illustrated by Yola.
Chile: Editorial Universitaria, 1974. 109p. ISBN 84-286-
0074-0. $7. Gr. 4-8.
    First book of the outstanding Papelucho series originally
published in Chile in 1947. A favorite of Chilean young
readers because of its natural style, Papelucho exemplifies
a normal boy and his ingenious thoughts and desires.
Written in diary style, Papelucho tells about his feelings
toward his family, going on vacations, getting into trouble
at boarding school, breaking a leg, etc. Truly delightful
reading about a normal boy that will amuse boys and girls.
Fluency in Spanish is important to understand this series.

Paz, Marcela. Papelucho casi huérfano [Papelucho Almost an

Orphan]. Chile: Editorial Universitaria, 1975. 89p.
ISBN 84-286-0075-9. $9. Gr. 4-8.

As soon as Papelucho's parents inherited a lot of money
from a rich uncle, they decide to take a trip to the United
States. Papelucho stays in Chile with an aunt; for this
reason he is almost an orphan. In his natural style, Papelucho tells about his sad feelings: he feels abandoned
by his parents, neglected by his aunt, and unwanted even
by gypsies. Everything is wonderful as soon as mother
returns.

Paz, Marcela. Papelucho detective [Papelucho Detective].
Chile: Editorial Universitaria, 1974. 120p. ISBN 84-286-
0008-2. $7. Gr. 4-8.

Papelucho is under arrest but not in prison, or so he
writes to his mother. His mother and father are very excited because she is expecting another baby. There are
problems with the pregnancy, so she must stay in bed.
Papelucho describes his feelings about a new sister, as
well as getting into trouble with his friends.

Paz, Marcela. Papelucho: diario secreto de Papelucho y el
marciano [Papelucho: Secret Diary of Papelucho and the
Martian]. Chile: Editorial Universitaria, 1976. 119p.
ISBN Unavailable. $7. Gr. 4-8.

In a secret diary, Papelucho tells his feelings about his
Martian friend who moves in with him. Papelucho's father
and mother tried to help, but secrecy is crucial. After
causing a great deal of excitement at home, Papelucho re-
covers from "bronchopneumonia" but his secret and the
Martian knowledge he gained stays with him.

Paz, Marcela. Papelucho en vacaciones [Papelucho on vaca-
tion]. Chile: Editorial Universitaria, 1974. 110p. ISBN
84-286-0088-0. $7. Gr. 4-8.

In the author's naturally animated style, Papelucho narrates his camping adventures with his father and mother.
Family quarrels and misunderstandings as well as Papelucho's
pranks with his friends are pleasingly described in another
Papelucho book.

Paz, Marcela. Papelucho historiador [Papelucho as Historian].
Chile: Editorial Universitaria, 1974. 99p. ISBN 84-286-
0079-1. $7. Gr. 4-8.
   Papelucho decides to rewrite the history of Chile so
that he may truly understand it. Continuing the author's
marvelously simple and amusing writing style, the reader
is exposed to the pre-Columbian Indians of Chile, the
Quechua; to the Spanish Conquistadores: to the Spanish
Colonial Period; and to the heroes who won Chile's independence. A tremendous book to introduce young readers
to the history of Spanish-speaking countries.

Paz, Marcela. Papelucho: mi hermana Ji [Papelucho: My
Sister Ji]. Chile: Editorial Universitaria, 1976. 96p.
ISBN Unavailable. $7. Gr. 4-8.
   In another delightful Papelucho book, a charming boy
describes his feelings about having a younger sister. Refreshing childish behavior and natural dialogues show the
daily life of a Chilean family, especially the trials of a boy
with a sister who goes to nursery school.

Paz, Marcela. Papelucho: mi hermano Hippie [Papelucho:
My Brother the Hippie]. Chile: Editorial Universitaria,
1975. 127p. ISBN 84-286-0080-5. $7. Gr. 4-8.
   Adventures of Papelucho as he tries to help his hippie
brother, Javier, survive while Javier attempts to save the
world. It is written in a very light manner, which may
attract boys whose Spanish vocabulary is quite extensive.
The incidents with Papelucho's teacher and new friend
Chori, who had never attended school, are amusing. Readers will need a strong knowledge of Spanish to enjoy Javier's return to his middle-class, old-fashioned family.

Paz, Marcela. Papelucho misionero [Papelucho as Missionary].
Chile: Editorial Universitaria, 1975. 120p. ISBN 84-286-
0082-1. $7. Gr. 4-8.
   Papelucho's father decides to go to Africa to search for
diamonds. Even though mother is concerned about Papelucho's and Javier's education, the family embarks on flight
623 to Dakar, Senegal. In a witty, amusing style Papelucho tells about flying on a plane, preparing for an international trip, arriving in a new country, failing to find any
diamonds, and returning home.

Paz, Marcela. Papelucho perdido [Lost Papelucho]. Chile:
Editorial Universitaria, 1974. 95p. ISBN 84-286-0087-2.
$7. Gr. 4-8.
During all the confusion at the train station, Papelucho
and his sister get on the wrong train going to Southern
Chile. The many ingenious adventures that Papelucho and
his younger sister go through in trying to locate their
missing parents are again charmingly described. Several
incidents show life on Chilean farms, as viewed by a boy
from the capital.

Pintado, Cecilio. El curricán [The Spinning Tackle]. Illustrated by Esdrujulus. Valladolid: Editorial Miñón, 1982.
136p. ISBN 84-355-0645-2. $6. Gr. 6-9.
Unexpectedly, a 12-year-old boy finds himself on a
yacht at sea. When a bad storm forces the yacht on a
different course, the young hero gains courage through
his imagined friend, a spinning tackle that was tied to the
yacht. Lovers of the sea will find excitement and adventure as well as a fond description of marine life in this
story, which takes place off the coast of Spain.

Posadas Mañé, Carmen de. Kiwi [Kiwi]. Illustrated by Antonio Tello. Madrid: Ediciones S.M., 1984. 61p. ISBN
84-348-1262-2. $3.50. Gr. 3-5.
This is an unusual animal story about a kiwi, a flight-
less bird of New Zealand. All the animals on the farm
were alarmed when the mailman delivered what they thought
was a dangerous thing. When they found out it was a big
egg, the old dog was the only one who volunteered to care
for it. But when the animals heard that a kiwi was born
and it would be famous all over the world, they rushed to
offer to take kiwi with them. The old dog, however, had
decided to be the kiwi's father and care for him. Amusing
two-tone, line illustrations of farm animals in various settings add a merry touch to this warm story of a dog with
strong paternal feelings.

Posadas Mañé, Carmen de. El señor Viento Norte [Mr. North
Wind]. Illustrated by Alfonso Ruano. Madrid: Ediciones
S.M., 1983. [26p.] ISBN 84-348-1225-8. $5. Gr. 3-5.
It was the month of March, and Mr. North Wind insisted

on blowing very hard. The animals of the forest got together and decided to do something about it. They went
to see Arturo and asked him for help. He volunteered to
see Mr. North Wind, deliver their gift, and ask him to allow spring to come in. Arturo and María, a brave girl,
finally convinced North Wind to blow south, and together
they saw the beginnings of spring. The alluring, pastel
illustrations are as captivating as the story.

Puncel, María. Clara y el caimán [Clara and the Alligator].
   Illustrated by Margarita Puncel. Madrid: Ediciones Altea,
   1983. [30p.] ISBN 84-372-1771-7. $4. Gr. 3-5.
      Clara was looking forward to her birthday, as her
   grandmother had promised to give her anything she wanted.
   That is how Clara got a baby alligator. At first, Clara
   eagerly took care of her pet. But after a few days her
   friends' excitement cooled down and Clara lost interest in
   her alligator. She didn't even notice when her grandmother
   accidentally lost the alligator. So, it was a great surprise
   to the scientific community when Clara and her grandmother
   went to identify the strange-looking alligator. Unpretentious, black-and-white illustrations add an amusing spark
   to this lighthearted story about a girl, her understanding
   grandmother, and a forgotten pet.

Puncel, María. Un hatillo de cerezas [A Bundle of Cherries].
   Illustrated by Viví Escrivá. Madrid: Ediciones S.M.,
   1984. [26p.] ISBN 84-348-1336-X. $6.50. Gr. 3-5.
      Antonio, a baker's helper, worked all night preparing
   the dough, heating up the oven and baking bread. One
   early morning as he set out to distribute the warm bread
   accompanied by his white mule, he met Tío Curro whose
   wagon was stuck in a big hole. Kindly, Antonio offered
   to help. Tío Curro was so grateful that he offered Antonio a bundle of beautiful red cherries. Antonio loved
   cherries but he thought of his grandmother Francisca who
   could only eat soft, juicy things, and he gave her the
   cherries. Grandmother Francisca loved cherries, but she
   thought of her sister who worked hard weaving clothes and
   gave her the cherries. Finally, the cherries made a full
   circle: Antonio got a bundle of cherries for dessert.
   Spectacular, watercolor illustrations of rural Spain are a
   beautiful complement to this touching story about giving,
   unaffected people.

Puncel, Mar\u00eda. **El prado del T\u00edo Pedro** [Uncle Peter's Meadow].
Illustrated by Teo Puebla. Madrid: Ediciones S.M., 1983.
[26p.] ISBN 84-348-1226-6. $4.50. Gr. 4-6.
When Uncle Peter died, he left a nice-looking meadow
and nine healthy sheep to his three sons and their wives.
At first, everybody was happy, caring for their sheep,
making cheeses, spinning wools, making clothes, and selling
their products. They started having serious problems
when one of the wives came up with an ambitious idea with
disastrous results. Eventually, the three brothers came
up with three different endings to their story. All three
endings are believable; one is ideal. The author makes an
interesting point, but allows young readers to disagree.
It is obvious to see why the beautiful watercolor illustrations in this book won the Spanish National Award for Illustrated Children's Books in 1982.

El rabipelado necesario [The Needed Porcupine]. Illustrated
by Carlos A. Chapman I. Caracas: R. J. Ediciones,
1984? [12p.] ISBN Unavailable. $3.50. Gr. 2-4.
The interrelationship between animals and plants is
aptly demonstrated through the experiences of a farmer
who got tired of the porcupines eating his hens. He later
realized that nature requires a balance to maintain itself.
Simple illustrations complement the text.

S\u00e1nchez, J. L. Garc\u00eda, and M. A. Pacheco. **Los ni\u00f1os que
no ten\u00edan escuelas** [Children Who Did Not Have Schools].
Illustrated by Nella Bosnia. Madrid: Ediciones Altea,
1984. [42p.] ISBN 84-372-1817-9. $3.50. Gr. 3-5.
Two ignorant mayors of two neighboring towns were
busy competing with each other. When one built a statue,
the other built a bigger one; when one built a huge stone
town hall, the other built a beautiful town hall made out
of crystal and marble, and so forth. They spent so much
money on grandiose schemes, that they didn't bother to
build schools. So, the children in both towns developed
a plan: They went to see their mayors and told them to
build a good school so that they could be more famous than
the other mayor. Thus both towns had beautiful new
schools where they finally sent their ignorant mayors. Attractive, watercolor illustrations beautifully complement this
story.

Sola, María Luisa. Ana [Ana]. Illustrated by Isidro Monés.
Barcelona: La Galera, 1980. 128p. ISBN 84-246-4516-2.
$8. Gr. 3-6.
    Ana's parents are doctors in Barcelona and have a maid
to do all the housework. Ana's feelings and thoughts are
very well described in a most enjoyable story of a typical
teenager in slacks, long hair, tennis racket, guitar and
records, who goes unwillingly to spend her summer holidays with her aunt, uncle, and cousins in the country.

Thurber, James. Muchas lunas [Many Moons]. Illustrated
by Juan Marchesi. Translated by J. Davis. Buenos Aires:
Ediciones de la Flor, 1983. 32p. ISBN Unavailable. $5.
Gr. 5-8.
    This Spanish translation of J. Thurber's Many Moons,
the story of a princess who wanted the moon, has maintained the flavor of the original English version. Unfortunately, the disfigured illustrations do not add much appeal to the story.

Turin, Adela. Las cajas de cristal [The Crystal Boxes]. Illustrated by Nella Bosnia. Translated by Humpty Dumpty.
Barcelona: Editorial Lumen, 1980. [36p.] ISBN 84-264-
3595-5. $4.50. Gr. 4-6.
    Well-written fantasy that tells about Asolina, a young
seamstress, who decides to see the world and ends up
saving two enchanted young maidens. Attractive illustrations complement the adventures of Asolina in the forest
and in the bewitched castle.

Turin, Adela, and Nella Bosnia. Una feliz catástrofe [A Happy
Catastrophe]. Translated by Humpty Dumpty. Barcelona:
Editorial Lumen, 1983? [34p.] ISBN 84-264-3515-3.
$8.50. Gr. 3-5.
    Mr. Mouse was a proud, strong husband and father.
Mrs. Mouse was a docile and obedient wife; they had eight
little mice. Before the catastrophe, Mr. Mouse told the
family exactly what to do and when. But, after the flood,
Mrs. Mouse reorganized the household and from then on
Mr. Mouse was in charge of cooking the soup. Bold, color-
ful illustrations of mice in various activities add an enjoyable touch to this somewhat modern family story.

Turin, Adela. El jardinero astrólogo [The Astrologer Garden-
er]. Illustrated by Barbara de Brunhoff. Translated by
Humpty Dumpty. Barcelona: Editorial Lumen, 1982.
[26p.] ISBN 84-264-3572-6. $4. Gr. 3-6.
  Delightful story about an astrologer gardener, a beautiful maiden, a wicked king, a young prince, and what
happens when the gardener misreads the stars' portent
about his newly born daughter. The intelligent maiden
prefers her life as an outstanding gardener to being married to the Prince of Sarcanda. Engaging illustrations
complement the fast-moving text.

Vanhalewijn, Mariette. La brujita Wanda [Wanda the Witch].
Illustrated by Jaklien Moerman. León: Editorial Everest,
1983. [32p.] ISBN 84-241-5352-9. $4. Gr. 3-6.
  Wanda, the youngest witch in the city of witches, often
bothered her mother with her mischief. So, when Wanda
"forgot" to get rid of a multitude of flies and 20 spiders,
her mother decided it was time to punish her: she sent
Wanda to live as a normal girl into the world with the ad-
monition that she couldn't return home until she did a good
deed. Most humans, however, wouldn't accept her because
she looked like a witch. Finally, a young boy suggested
that Wanda help his mother peel five buckets of potatoes,
and thus Wanda was allowed to return home. "[... And
from then on Wanda really tried to be good.]" Unfortunate
ending mars an otherwise interesting story about a young
witch with beautiful, colorful illustrations.

Vanhalewijn, Mariette. El gato sabio de Juanito [Little John's
Wise Cat]. Illustrated by Jaklien Moerman. León: Editorial Everest, 1983. [32p.] ISBN 84-241-5351-0. $4.
Gr. 3-5.
  Juanito, a seven-year-old boy, found a gray kitten in
his back yard. He very much wanted to keep the kitten,
but his father was afraid that the kitten would eat their
neighbor's canaries. His mother did not want kitten's
hairs in her nice sofas, his brother did not trust cats,
and his sister feared that the kitten would eat her fish.
So, Juanito negotiated with kitten and finally got him to
"sign" a note promising that he would not do any of these
things, even though kitten wondered how he could be happy.
Gray kitten solved his problem by once in a while going

out for a "day of adventure." Delightful, colorful illustrations complement the captivating story about a boy and his
feelings about his kitten.

Vanhalewijn, Mariette. Los 365 vestidos de la princesa Penélope [Princess Penélope's 365 Dresses]. Illustrated by
Jaklien Moerman. León: Editorial Everest, 1983. 32p.
ISBN 84-241-5354-5. $4. Gr. 3-5.
     Penélope, a beautiful princess, had one defect: she
felt she had to wear a new dress every day. Her mother,
the queen, tried to reason with her, but nobody could
convince Penélope that wearing a new dress every day
wasn't necessary. The king decided to end Penélope's un-
reasonable demand and stopped the production of new
dresses for his daughter. This caused the princess much
pain, and she cried and cried. Tomasita, a maid's daughter, heard her and tried to comfort her. The princess
suggested that they exchange the dress Tomasita was
wearing for any one of the princess' dresses. Thus,
Penélope realized that an old dress could be pretty too.
Attractive, colorful illustrations of a lively princess at
court enliven the entertaining text.

Vázquez-Vigo, Carmen. Caramelos de menta [Mint Caramels].
Illustrated by Antonio Tello. Madrid: S. M. Ediciones,
1981. 132p. ISBN 84-325-0442-4. $13. Gr. 6-8.
     Four boys and one girl must come up with money to
pay for damages to the owner of a chicken and egg store,
which were caused by their newly-found dog, Dragon.
They try everything they can think of--selling candy, de-
livering baked goods, playing football, entering dog con-
tests--but they don't have enough money. Surprisingly,
Dragon finds his previous owner, who is delighted to give
them the money to pay for the damages, as well as to get
the boys the things they most wanted: a skeleton, a soccer ball, and cakes.
     The unaffected style of this author, as well as the en-
tertaining dialogue, makes this story a refreshing encounter with Spanish young people.

Vázquez-Vigo, Carmen. El muñeco de don Bepo [Don Bepo's
Doll]. Illustrated by Arcadio Lobato. Madrid: Ediciones
S.M., 1984. 64p. ISBN 84-348-1287-8. $4. Gr. 3-6.

Don Bepo, a ventriloquist, decides to retire to his village in Spain. He can't find a better use for Ruperto, his dummy, so he plants him as a scarecrow in the middle of his orchard. Ruperto prefers to see the world and asks Verdurina, a peasant fairy, to give him the power to move his legs. Ruperto's experiences in the city are quite discouraging, so he returns home where Don Bepo is preparing a ventriloquist show for the children in town. The amusing three-tone line illustrations add a nice touch of merriment to the life of Don Bepo and his dummy, Ruperto.

Vázquez-Vigo, Carmen. El rey que voló [The King Who Flew]. Illustrated by Karin Schubert. Madrid: Ediciones Altea, 1980. 29p. ISBN 84-372-1483-1. $5. Gr. 3-6.
This is a delightful story about a wicked king who burdened his court with his incessant demands. On the one thousandth anniversary of the foundation of his kingdom, he decided to have an elaborate celebration. He ordered a new dancing hall, extravagant parades, and the most majestic long, wide gown ever made. The court tailor panicked, as he knew how difficult to please the king was. However, his courageous friend, Alicia, helped him, and the gown was finished on time. The king's reactions to the gown and a mysterious prank played by another tailor keep this story exciting until the end when Alicia and her friends get rid of the ungrateful king. Amusing, colorful illustrations complement the easy-to-read text.

Walsh, María Elena. El diablo inglés [The English Devil]. Illustrated by Raúl Fortin. Buenos Aires: Angel Estrada y Cia, 1974. 16p. ISBN Unavailable. $3. Gr. 2-5.
Delightful illustrations and charming text tell the story of the English devils that appeared in Argentina in 1806. Tomás, an Argentinian young man, is scared by the appearance of an English soldier, who he confused with the devil. Tomás consults his friend, the witch Manuela, who agrees with his fears. This is a witty story that alludes to the English invasion of Argentina in 1806.

Walsh, María Elena. El país de la geometría [Land of Geometry]. Illustrated by Néstor Luis Battagliero. Buenos Aires: Editorial Estrada, 1974. 18p. ISBN Unavailable. $3. Gr. 3-6.

Amusing story which uses geometric designs and illustrations about the King of the Compass who was unhappily
searching for his round flower. Simple dialogues and
charming illustrations engage the reader into geometric
concepts.

Wilde, Oscar. El príncipe feliz [The Happy Prince]. Illus-
trated by Joanna Isles. Translated by José Emilio Pacheco.
México: Promexa, 1982. [28p.] ISBN 968-34-0171-6. $3.
Gr. 5-8.
Delightful version in Spanish of Wilde's The Happy
Prince with striking watercolor illustrations.

Wildsmith, Brian. El arca espacial del profesor Noé [Professor
Noah's Spaceship]. Translated by José Emilio Pacheco.
México: Asuri de Ediciones, 1982. [32p.] ISBN 968-34-
0172-4. $5. Gr. 3-6.
Professor Noah's Spaceship, originally published in England in 1908, is a twentieth-century version of animals in
search of a home on Earth which is free of pollution. The
attractive, colorful illustrations and an easy-flowing Spanish text will appeal to Spanish readers.

EASY BOOKS

Altamirano, Francisca. El niño y el globo [The Boy and the Balloon]. Illustrated by the author. México: Editorial Trillas, 1985. 12p. ISBN 968-24-1845-3. $3.50. Gr. K-2.
   This wordless picture book shows a boy and his big blue balloon in the city, in the sky, in the country, over the ocean, over snowcapped mountains, and on a tree. The striking illustrations will attract children's attention.

Amarillo girasol [Yellow Flower]. ISBN 968-24-1539-X.

Arco iris [Rainbow]. ISBN 968-24-1543-8.

Azul marino [Navy Blue]. ISBN 968-24-1535-7.

Azul rey [King Blue]. ISBN 968-24-1533-0.

Blanco aparicio [White]. ISBN 968-24-1537-3.

Marrón ratón [Brown Mouse]. ISBN 968-24-1540-3.

Naranja limpión [Orange]. ISBN 968-24-1542-X.

Negra escobilla [Black]. ISBN 968-24-1541-1.

Púrpura candido [Purple]. ISBN 968-24-1532-2.

Roja sorpresa [Surprise Red]. ISBN 968-24-1538-1.

Roso ronquillo [Pink]. ISBN 968-24-1534-9.

132 Basic Collection of Books in Spanish

Verde gruñón [Grumpy Green]. ISBN 968-24-1536-5.

Ea. vol.: 32p. México: Editorial Trillas, 1983. (Serie Manchitas). $5. Gr. 3-5.
The small size (5" x 6½") and colorful format of this series originally published in England may appeal to reluctant readers. There is a special vibrancy in this series about 12 luminous blobs that come out of their paint box into the marvelous world of colors. Thus, children will find out how yellow primrose made the king happy, purple puppy became a sailor, royal blue painted everything blue, ghostly white found his perfect job, mousy brown found his way home, and other lighthearted predicaments.

Amo, Montserrat Del. Chitina y su gato [Chitina and Her Cat]. Illustrated by María Rius. Barcelona: Juventud, 1976. 16p. ISBN 84-261-0935-7. $4. Gr. K-2.
Splendid illustrations and simple, lively text combine to make this story about Chitina and her cat a truly enjoyable animal story for young children.

Armijo, Consuelo. Moné [Moné]. Illustrated by Montse Ginesta. Valladolid: Editorial Miñón, S.A., 1982. [26p.] ISBN 84-355-0633-9. $3. Gr. 2-4.
Moné is a good and kind teddy bear. He is a trustworthy companion always willing to play with lonely or sad children. Handsome illustrations complement this affectionate story of children and their favorite toy.

Balzola, Asun. Munia y el cocolilo naranja [Munia and the Orange "Clocodile"]. ISBN 84-233-1335-2.

_____. Munia y la señora Piltronera [Munia and Mrs. Piltronera]. ISBN 84-233-1290-9.

Ea. vol.: 27p. Illustrated by the author. (Algunas veces Munia). Barcelona: Ediciones Destino, 1984. $10. Gr. 2-4.
Like previous Munia stories, these new titles describe the genuine feelings and worries of Munia, a little girl who lives with her parents and sister in a small village in Spain. Delicate watercolor-pastel illustrations with a modern accent

set an honest mood to these stories. Munia y la señora
Piltronera is the more touching of the two stories. It
tells about Munia's feelings of anger and hostility when
things don't seem to go well during a whole day. Finally,
she dresses like Mrs. Piltronera and confronts her parents
with the difficult question: Do you still love your naughty
daughter, Munia?   The results are a happy smiling Munia.
Munia y el cocolilo naranja describes Munia's fears when
she started losing her teeth. One day she lost one and
very soon another one. Her parents tried to reassure her,
but she was sure that she was not going to have teeth for
the rest of her life. One night she dreamed that an orange
crocodile, who also did not have teeth, would defend her
from all the bad crocodiles in the world. After a long discussion about crocodiles in Egypt, Munia fell asleep. One
day Munia felt a new tooth and said good-by to her friend,
the orange "clocodile."

Balzola, Asun. Munia y la luna [Munia and the Moon]. Il-
    lustrated by Eugenia Alcorta and Rosaura Martínez. Bar-
    celona: Ediciones Destino, 1982. [24p.] ISBN 84-233-
    1199-6. $10. Gr. 1-3.
    Munia, a little girl, lived with her family in a little
house on the top of a mountain. One early evening they
ran out of water so they had to go down to the river to
get some. Munia filled up a bottle of water with the moon's
face in it. That night she dreamt that the moon asked
her to return the little piece of moon she had taken away
so that the moon could shine again.
    Simple story with unsophisticated illustrations about a
little girl, the moon, and her dreams.

Balzola, Asun. Los zapatos de Munia [Munia's Shoes]. Bar-
    celona: Ediciones Destino, 1983. 23p. ISBN 84-233-
    1243-7. $8.95. Gr. 2-4.
    Munia, a little girl, lived in the country. One day,
she was eager to go into town, but her mother and father
were busy and didn't want to go. Finally, she found a
neighbor who needed to go into town and who was willing
to take her and bring her back home. Thus, Munia put
on her shoes and rode into town. As soon as she got
there, Munia ran to the shoemaker and explained her problem to him: She had been extra careful with her shoes,

but her shoes had shrunk and now she was worried that
her parents would scold her. The shoemaker kindly explained to her that children grow up and that it wasn't
the shoes that had shrunk, but rather her feet had grown.
Munia was delighted because now her parents would buy
her a new pair of shoes. Delicate pastel illustrations of
Munia in her difficult predicament beautifully complement
this touching story of a girl genuinely worried about her
shoes.

Barbot, Daniel. Un diente se mueve [A Tooth Moves]. Illustrated by Gian Calvi. Caracas: Ediciones Ekaré-Banco
del Libro, 1981. [24p.] ISBN Unavailable. $4. Gr. 1-3.
    Clarisse, a little girl, was worried about losing her
first tooth. She had heard that a mouse would come to
take her tooth. So, the day she lost her tooth, she put
it under her pillow just before going to sleep. That night
she had a marvelous dream; when she woke up the next
morning, she found a coin instead of her tooth, and she
realized she was not dreaming at all. Colorful, although
somewhat coarse, illustrations adequately supplement the
text.

Benet, Amelia. Silvia y Miguel en verano [Silvia and Miguel
in the Summer]. Illustrated by Rosa Rius. Barcelona:
Juventud, 1970. 14p. ISBN 84-261-0899-7. $3. Gr. K-
2.
    Attractive illustrations show Spanish children in their
summer activities: the Fiesta de San Juan, visits to the
countryside, school parties, parks, holiday preparations,
and trips to the beach.

Burningham, John. La alacena [The Cupboard]. ISBN 968-
39-0050-X.

_____. El amigo [The Friend]. ISBN 968-39-0049-6.

_____. El bebé [The Baby]. ISBN 968-39-0051-8.

_____. La cobija [The Blanket]. ISBN 968-39-0048-8.

_____. El conejo [The Rabbit]. ISBN 968-39-0046-1.

_____. La escuela [The School]. ISBN 968-39-0047-X.

_____. El perro [The Dog]. ISBN 968-39-0045-3.

Ea. vol.: 20p. (Serie Pre-Escolar Bilingüe). México:
Editorial Patria, 1984. $3. Gr. PK-2.
This charming series about a little boy's experiences at
home and at school was originally published in England in
1974. Simple pastel illustrations and an easy-to-read bilingual (Spanish and English) text show a curious little
boy exploring a kitchen cupboard; telling about his friend,
Arthur, a new baby at home, his favorite blanket, his
black rabbit, a neighbor's dog, and a day in school. The
ingenious illustrations and commonplace situations described
should make this series of special interest to the very
young. Some adults (in the U.S.) might object to the
small size (6" x 6") of these publications and to the British spelling in the English text.

Capdevila, Juan. Nico y Ana en el campo [Nico and Ana at
the Farm]. Illustrated by Violeta Denou. Barcelona:
Editorial Timun Mas, 1979? 28p. ISBN 84-7176-341-9.
$3. Gr. K-3.
Simple text and charming illustrations describe Nico's
and Ana's visit to a farm. The farmer takes them for a
ride in a tractor. They also play in the orchards, collect
freshly laid eggs, eat homemade bread and cheese, and for
dessert they get a sweet and refreshing watermelon. They
return home with many gifts for the family: fruits, vegetables, hens, and a duck. Delightful story about life on
a farm.

Capdevila, Juan. Nico y Ana hacen fotos [Nico and Ana Make
Photographs]. Illustrated by Violeta Denou. Barcelona:
Editorial Timun Mas, 1979? 28p. ISBN 84-7176-342-7.
$3. Gr. 1-3.
Nico and Ana decide to learn about photography. They
watch a photographer at work at a wedding, at a fashion
show, at a portrait studio, at a ballet academy, and at a
soccer game. The photographer teaches them how to take
their own pictures. They also learn to work in the lab.
The simple text and charming illustrations will certainly delight young readers and will entice them into the world of
photography.

Capdevila, Juan. Nico y Ana quieren ser bomberos [Nico and
Ana Want to Be Firemen]. Illustrated by Violeta Denou.
Barcelona: Editorial Timun Mas, 1979? 28p. ISBN 84-
7176-315-X. $3. Gr. K-3.
   When the stove at Nico and Ana's kitchen catches fire,
they call the firemen and decide to become firefighters.
They are introduced to the work of firefighters by watching them in their daily training exercises, by accompanying them to extinguish a fire aboard a ship and at a forest. They also assist an artist whose house was flooded
and some neighbors whose house was on fire. They demonstrate how much they've learned by rescuing a neighbor's
cat from a roof. Simple text and attractive illustrations
introduce young readers to firefighters and their work.

Capdevila, Juan. Nico y Ana quieren ser médicos [Nico and
Ana Want to Be Doctors]. Illustrated by Violeta Denou.
Barcelona: Editorial Timun Mas, 1979? 28p. ISBN 84-
7176-313-3. $3. Gr. 2-4.
   At a picnic with their family, Nico and Ana fall from a
tree and must be taken to a nearby hospital. After they
are treated for minor injuries, they begin to think that it
must be a good thing to cure people. Nico walks through
the hospital, and a young doctor invites him to watch an
operation. They play doctor games and go to the university to visit the School of Medicine. Upon returning home,
they see a dog with a broken leg and decide to cure him.
They are happy with their first patient. Simple text and
attractive illustrations introduce young readers to the world
of doctors.

Capdevila, Juan. Nico y Ana quieren ser músicos [Nico and
Ana Want to Be Musicians]. Illustrated by Violeta Denou.
Barcelona: Editorial Timun Mas, 1979? 28p. ISBN 84-
7176-314-1. $3. Gr. 1-3.
   Simple text and amusing illustrations tell about Nico and
Ana's introduction to the world of music and musicians.
They are shown performing at a school concert, enjoying
the town's band at a city square, listening to an orchestra
at a concert hall, visiting opera singers backstage, and
attending their first music lessons at the conservatory.
Young readers will enjoy this introduction to musicians and
their work.

Capdevila, Juan. Teo en avión [Teo on an Airplane]. Illustrated by Violeta Denou. Barcelona: Editorial Timun Mas,
1980. 32p. ISBN 84-7176-258-7. $5. Gr. 1-3.
Teo describes his first airplane trip: the airport, the
pilot and copilot, a parachute, sleeping on the plane,
dreaming about Mars, eating on the plane, etc. Busy,
colorful illustrations complement the story.

Capdevila, Juan. Teo en barco [Teo on a Ship]. Illustrated
by Violeta Denou. Barcelona: Editorial Timun Mas, 1980.
32p. ISBN 84-7176-257-9. $5. Gr. 1-3.
Teo is playing at the beach and finds a message invit-
ing him to visit an island. The ship is getting ready to
leave. Teo describes his experiences traveling by ship as
well as his arrival at the tropical island. Colorful illustrations depict ship and ocean scenes.

Capdevila, Juan. Teo en el circo [Teo at the Circus]. Illustrated by Violeta Denou. Barcelona: Editorial Timun
Mas, 1980. 32p. ISBN 84-7176-270-6. $5. Gr. 1-3.
The circus arrives in town and Teo and his friends go
to watch the preparations. They play with the animals,
and they observe various acrobats during their training.
When the program begins, they are delighted with an ele-
plant show, acrobats, white horses, magicians, gymnasts,
and finally clowns. Gay, colorful circus illustrations complement the simple text.

Capdevila, Juan. Teo en la escuela [Teo at School]. Illustrated by Violeta Denou. Barcelona: Editorial Timun Mas,
1979. 32p. ISBN 84-7176-311-7. $5. Gr. 1-3.
Teo is shown at school, where he is involved in various
activities such as art classes, physical education, lunch
time, rest time, music lessons, a field trip to a museum,
and a puppet show. Simple text and colorful illustrations
depict children in a school setting in a most enjoyable
manner.

Capdevila, Juan. Teo en la nieve [Teo in the Snow]. Illustrated by Violeta Denou. Barcelona: Editorial Timun Mas,
1980. 32p. ISBN 84-7176-343-5. $5. Gr. 1-3.

Amid happy winter scenes, Teo describes his skiing experiences with his friends and teachers. They are shown arriving at a winter cottage, spending an evening by the fireplace, playing in the snow, making a snowman, learning to ice skate, going for a sleigh ride, and skiing down a big mountain.

Capdevila, Juan. Teo en tren [Teo on a Train]. Illustrated by Violeta Denou. Barcelona: Editorial Timun Mas, 1980. 32p. ISBN 84-7176-256-0. $5. Gr. 1-3.

Teo discovers an abandoned train engine. So, he convinces his uncle, Luis, to take the whole family on a vacation. They go through the city, a gypsy camp, a pasture, a farm, over a river, inside a tunnel, and they finally arrive at the mountains to spend their vacation. Attractive, colorful illustrations depict train and nature scenes.

Capdevila, Juan. Teo y su familia [Teo and His Family]. Illustrated by Violeta Denou. Barcelona: Editorial Timun Mas, 1980. 32p. ISBN 84-7176-312-5. $5. Gr. 1-3.

Teo and his family get ready for Christmas vacation which they will spend with his grandparents, aunts, uncles, and cousins. Colorful illustrations and a simple text show papa at work at his bakery, mama caring for baby, Teo setting the table while papa fixes dinner, and finally all the family getting ready for the trip to the country to celebrate Christmas.

Chapouton, Anne-Marie. Los Bambalinos celebran la Navidad [The Bambalinos Celebrate Christmas]. ISBN 84-241-5220-4.

_____. Los Bambalinos y el elixir de sol [The Bambalinos and the Sun's Elixir]. ISBN 84-241-5219-0.

_____. Los Bambalinos y las ranas [The Bambalinos and the Frogs]. ISBN 84-241-5218-2.

Ea. vol.: Illustrated by Gerda Muller. Translated by Angel García Aller. 30p. León: Editorial Everest, 1983. $4.95. Gr. 2-4.

Bambalinos are tiny people that live in the forest. They work and play together. Los Bambalinos celebran la Navi-

dad shows how they prepare their "midnight suns" candy
and cakes and celebrate Christmas with some hungry mice.
In Los Bambalinos y el elixir de sol, Muroncito, their wise
magician, helps the Bambalinos happily survive a long winter by making a delicious sun's elixir. Los Bambalinos y
las ranas shows how three "bambaniños," Gogo, Laura and
Quico, become good friends with the up-to-now feared
frogs. The outstanding presentation of these books--de-
lightful color illustrations, excellent paper, attractive
covers--add a tremendous appeal to these stories about
tiny, kind-hearted people.

Charles, Donald. El año de Gato Galano [Calico Cat's Year].
Translated by Alma Flor Ada. ISBN 0-516-33461-1.

_____. Cuenta con Gato Galano [Count on Calico Cat].
Translated by Lada Kratky. ISBN 0-516-33479-4.

_____. El libro de ejercicios de Gato Galano [Calico Cat's
Exercise Book]. Translated by Lada Kratky. ISBN 0-
516-33457-3.

Ea. vol.: 32p. Illustrated by the author. (Calico Cat
Storybook Series). Chicago: Childrens Press, 1984.
$8.25. Gr. Pre-School-2.
Each of these stories includes amusing, colorful illustrations of Calico Cat involved in activities that young children can readily understand. El año de Gato Galano describes, in a rhymed text in Spanish, the characteristics
of the four seasons. Cuenta con Gato Galano is a simple
counting book based on Calico Cat's garbage can. El
libro de ejercicios de Gato Galano shows Calico Cat demon-
strating various simple exercises to four mice. These books
will entertain as well as instruct young Spanish-speaking
children.

Company, Mercè. Bamba, el rey gordo [Bamba, the Fat King].
Illustrated by Agustí Asensio. Madrid: Ediciones Alfaguara,
S.A., 1982. 35p. ISBN 84-204-3060-9. $7. Gr. 2-4.
Bamba, the fat king, was very fat because he loved to
eat. Every day he ate three chickens, two rabbits, 25
oranges, one cake, two ice-cream dishes, and some peanuts.
The court magician warned him that he should lose weight.

But Bamba could not stop eating. When he sat on the throne and broke it, he realized he could not continue eating in excess. Delightful illustrations complement this good-natured story about a fat king.

D'Atri, Adriana. Así es nuestra casa [This Is Our House]. Illustrated by Ulises Wensell. Madrid: Ediciones Altea, 1980. 32p. ISBN 84-372-1298-7. $5. Gr. K-2.
A seven-year-old girl and her six-year-old brother in-terestingly describe their house: the dining room that was converted into a much-needed bedroom, the hallway as an ideal place to play, the bedroom beds that mama said shouldn't be destroyed, the cluttered bathroom, and the many repairs that need to be done. The brief and simple text and the enchanting illustrations will delight young children and also readers who are learning Spanish as a second language.

D'Atri, Adriana. Así es nuestro hermano pequeño [This Is Our Baby Brother]. Illustrated by Ulises Wensell. Madrid: Ediciones Altea, 1980. 32p. ISBN 84-372-1303-7. $5. Gr. K-2.
A seven-year-old girl and her six-year-old brother charmingly tell about their baby brother. They fondly describe various times and details in their lives, from the moment that the baby was brought home from the hospital until he can walk on the beach holding mama's hand. The brief and simple text and the enchanting illustrations will delight young children.

D'Atri, Adriana. Así es nuestro perro [This Is Our Dog]. Illustrated by Ulises Wensell. Madrid: Ediciones Altea, 1980. 32p. ISBN 84-372-1304-5. $5. Gr. K-2.
A seven-year-old girl and her six-year-old brother de-scribe their black dog, Carbón. Carbón arrived at their home when it was only two-weeks old, and the children re-count many experiences with their dog: visits to friends' homes, fights with a parrot, learning to do tricks with their father, visits to the veterinarian, etc. The brief and simple text will delight young children and also read-ers who are learning Spanish as a second language.

D'Atri, Adriana. Así pasamos el día [This Is the Way We
Spent Our Day]. Illustrated by Ulises Wensell. Madrid:
Ediciones Altea, 1980. 32p. ISBN 84-372-1297-9. $5.
Gr. K-2.
    A seven-year-old girl and her six-year-old brother
charmingly describe one day in their family's life: taking
the school bus, painting and eating at school, visiting a
bakery shop, visiting grandparents, visiting neighbors,
going to the park, going to the doctor, etc. The brief
and simple text and the enchanting illustrations will delight
young children.

D'Atri, Adriana. Así somos nosotros [This Is the Way We Are].
Illustrated by Ulises Wensell. Madrid: Ediciones Altea,
1980. 32p. ISBN 84-372-1300-2. $5. Gr. K-2.
    Clara, a seven-year-old girl, and her six-year-old
brother, Enrique, tell about their lives: their visits to
the park, their quarrels, their school, their daily activities at home, their baby brother, their parents and grandparents. The brief and simple text and the enchanting
illustrations will delight young children and also readers
who are learning Spanish as their second language.

D'Atri, Adriana. Así son los abuelos que viven cerca [These
Are Our Grandparents Who Live Near]. Illustrated by
Ulises Wensell. Madrid: Ediciones Altea, 1980. 32p.
ISBN 84-372-1301-0. $5. Gr. K-2.
    A seven-year-old girl and her six-year-old brother de-
lightfully describe their grandparents that live nearby.
They tell about Grandma's baking and visit to the beauty
shop, and Grandpa's fishing and mechanic garage. They
tell about the fun they have together. The brief and simple
text and enchanting illustrations will delight young children.

D'Atri, Adriana. Así son los abuelos que viven lejos [These
Are Our Grandparents Who Live Far Away]. Illustrated by
Ulises Wensell. Madrid: Ediciones Altea, 1980. 32p.
ISBN 84-372-1296-0. $5. Gr. K-2.
    A seven-year-old girl and her six-year-old brother
charmingly describe their grandparents, who live far away.
They have a big two-story home with a big yard. Grand-
father is an architect who loves to paint whatever the chil-

dren ask him to. Grandmother loves music and going to
concerts. The children love going to visit them. The
brief and simple text and the enchanting illustrations will
delight young children.

D'Atri, Adriana. Así son los tíos [These Are Our Aunt and
Uncle]. Illustrated by Ulises Wensell. Madrid: Ediciones
Altea, 1980. 32p. ISBN 84-372-1299-5. $5. Gr. K-2.
   A seven-year-old girl and her six-year-old brother
charmingly tell us about their aunt, Isabel, and their
uncle, Jorge. They describe various activities they enjoy
doing together as well as their aunt's and uncle's occupations. The brief and simple text will delight young children.

D'Atri, Adriana. Así son nuestros amigos [These Are Our
Friends]. Illustrated by Ulises Wensell. Madrid: Ediciones Altea, 1980. 32p. ISBN 84-372-1302-9. $5. Gr.
K-2.
   A seven-year-old girl and her six-year-old brother
charmingly tell about their friends as well as their parents'
friends, their aunt's and uncle's friends, their grandparents' friends, and even their dog's friends. The brief
and simple text and enchanting illustrations will delight
young children.

D'Atri, Adriana. Así son papá y mamá [These Are Our Father and Mother]. Illustrated by Ulises Wensell. Madrid:
Ediciones Altea, 1980. 32p. ISBN 84-372-1305-3. $5.
Gr. K-2.
   A seven-year-old girl and her six-year-old brother
charmingly tell about their father and mother. Both of
them work; Papa is an engineer, and Mama is a dentist.
Both share life with their children, as well as various
housekeeping chores. They are shown in various work
and fun activities. The brief and simple text will delight
young children.

Delgado, Eduardo. Mientras Tim juega en el campo [While Tim
Plays in the Country]. ISBN 84-344-0153-3.

_____. Mientras Tim juega en los grandes almacenes
[While Tim Plays in the Big Department Stores]. ISBN
84-344-0215-7.

Ea. vol.: [20p.] Illustrated by Francesc Rovira.
(Colección Mientras Tim Juega). Barcelona: Editorial
Ariel, 1984. $5.50. Gr. 1-3.
Witty, busy, colorful illustrations with a lot of detail
are the salient characteristics of this amusing series with
simple texts which shows Tim, a little boy, getting involved
in preposterous situations. Mientras Tim juega en el campo
shows Tim and his friends going to the town's market and
taking with them some of their treasures. This results in
strange occurrences in the town's square, but lots of fun
for everybody. Mientras Tim juega en los grandes almacenes tells about Tim's experiences when he volunteered
to help others move a big piano in a busy department
store. Moving the piano in the store causes mass confusion and minor calamities. Ultimately, the piano is placed
in a nice, quiet terrace to provide background music to
the customers. Other titles in this series are: Mientras
Tim juega en el parque de atracciones [While Tim Plays in
the Amusement Park], Mientras Tim juega en la playa
[While Tim Plays at the Beach], Mientras Tim juega en el
puerto [While Tim Plays at the Port], Mientras Tim juega
e la plaza [While Tim Plays in the Plaza].

Denou, Violeta. Los animales de Teo [Teo's Animals]. Barcelona: Editorial Timun Mas, 1984? [10p.] ISBN 84-7176-
   519-5. $4. Gr. PK-2.
   Sturdy board pages and bright colorful illustrations are
ideal to tell young children about Teo and his animals,
which include caterpillars, turtles, a puppy, a parrot, and
a fish. This wordless picture book is a charming introduction to animals.

Denou, Violeta. Es navidad, Teo [It's Christmas, Teo]. Barcelona: Timun Mas, 1985? [10p.] ISBN 84-7176-666-3.
   $4. Gr. Pre-School-1.
   Colorful illustrations on sturdy cardboard pages show
happy scenes related to Christmas. This wordless picture
book includes children with Santa Claus, setting up a nativi-
ty scene, talking to a wise man, opening their gifts, and

removing the decorations from the Christmas tree. Hispanic Christmas celebrations are simply presented in this
attractive, durable book. Other "Teo" titles are: Teo
come [Teo Eats], Teo juega [Teo Plays], Llueve Teo [It
Is Raining, Teo], Los animales de Teo [Teo's Animals].

Denou, Violeta. Llueve, Teo [It Is Raining, Teo]. Illustrated
by the author. Barcelona: Editorial Timun Mas, 1983.
[10p.] ISBN 84-7176-520-9. $4. Gr. Pre-Schook-K.
Delightful, colorful illustrations and sturdy board pages
with no text show children what happens when it rains as
well as the special clothes children wear in the rain. These
illustrations of children and animals in the rain and under
a rainbow are sure to appeal to preschoolers.

Denou, Violeta. Teo en la feria [Teo at the Fair]. ISBN 84-
7176-525-X.

_____. Teo en tren [Teo on the Train]. ISBN 84-7176-
256-0.

_____. Teo y su perro [Teo and His Dog]. ISBN 84-7176-
430-X.

Ea. vol.: [28p.] Illustrated by the author. (Colección
Teo Descubre el Mundo). Barcelona: Editorial Timun Mas,
1983? $4. Gr. 1-3.
These are three more titles of the delightful series Teo
Discovers the World. Like their predecessors, these books
include gay, colorful illustrations and simple texts. Teo
en la feria shows Teo enjoying rides on the merry-go-
round and a small airplane, fishing for turtles, watching
a show about witches, eating candy, and other fun activities. Teo en tren tells about Teo's train ride with his
family on their way to their mountain cabin. Attractive
scenes of rural Spain add interest to Teo's train ride.
Teo y su perro shows Teo's adventures with his new puppy.
Children will delight in reading about Teo's varied and
amusing activities as depicted in the 15 books that comprise
this series to date.

Eastman, P. D. Perro grande ... perro pequeño [Big Dog

... Little Dog]. Translated into Spanish by Pilar de
Cuenca and Inés Alvarez. New York: Random House,
1982. [32p.] ISBN 0-394-05142-5. $9. Gr. K-2.
   Two dogs are very good friends yet opposite in every
way and do not know how to solve a mutual problem.
Thanks to a bird who realizes that we should not "make
big problems out of little problems," they simply changed
beds and resolved their sleeping problems. The amusing
and brief Spanish text is immediately followed by the English translation on every page. English version originally
published in 1973.

Escofet, Cristina. Llueve en la ciudad [It's Raining in the
   City]. Illustrated by Susana Bottega. Buenos Aires:
   Editorial Plus Ultra, 1981. [26p.] ISBN Unavailable. $3.
   Gr. 1-3.
   Pleasing rhymes and illustrations tell what happens
when it rains in the city: a cat catches a cold, a lady
gets wet, a car gets pneumonia, the city streets become
canals, the fruits are delighted.
   The simplicity of these rhymes makes this story an excellent introduction to the subject of rain as well as entertaining reading.

Fernández, Laura. Mariposa [Butterfly]. Illustrated by the
   author. México: Editorial Trillas, 1983. 16p. ISBN 968-
   24-1555-1. $3. Gr. 1-3.
   Butterfly was always bragging to her friends that she
could fly like the clouds and play with the wind. Her
friends--the other butterflies--didn't believe her and decided to test her. Afraid of failing, she asked a little
boy for help. When she flew up to the sky, the boy threw
her a long string and she became a kite. Since then butterflies fly without fear and children play with kites. The
colorful illustrations are the best part of this story.

Franca, Mary, and Eliardo Franca. Rabo de gato [Cat's Tail].
   Translated by Verónica Uribe. Caracas: Ediciones Ekaré-
   Banco del Libro, 1979. 10p. ISBN Unavailable. $3. Gr.
   K-2.
   Simply story about a toad that put on a cat's tail. An
armadillo saw him and called him a cat; a cat saw him and

called him a toad. But when a female toad asked him what
he was, he asserted three times: "I am a toad." Cheerful illustrations complement this brief and amusing story.

Friskey, Margaret. Pollito Pequeñito cuenta hasta diez [Chick-
en Little Counts to Ten]. Illustrated by Katherine Evans.
Translated by Lada Kratky. Chicago: Children's Press,
1984. [30p.] ISBN 0-516-33431-X. $8.25. Gr. 1-3.
     The popular Chicken Little, who sets out to see the
world but doesn't know how to drink water, is now available to Spanish-speaking children. Pollito Pequeñito (Chick-
en Little) learns how ten different animals get a drink, and
at the same time, counts from one to ten.

Gorostiza, Carlos. El barquito viajero [The Traveling Boat].
Illustrated by Blanca Medda. Buenos Aires: Editorial
Kapelusz, 1978. 14p. ISBN Unavailable. $3. Gr. 1-3.
     Amusing rhymes and attractive illustrations tell the
story of a little boat that goes out to sea. The passengers
get ready to board, its crew makes all the preparations,
and the people who stay behind wave good-by. There is
also a captain who is in charge, and finally the arrival to
a new port.

Gorostiza, Carlos. ¡Todos al zoológico! [Everyone to the
Zoo!]. Illustrated by Blanca Medda. Buenos Aires: Editorial Kapelusz, 1978. 14p. ISBN Unavailable. $3. Gr.
1-3.
     Simple and witty rhymes tell about a child's visit to
the zoo. It includes amusing descriptions and colorful illustrations of an elephant, a camel, a monkey, a peacock,
a lion, a giraffe, a polar bear, and a hippopotamus.

Granata, María. El bichito de luz sin luz [The Beetle Without
a Light]. Illustrated by Raul Stevano. Buenos Aires:
Editorial Sigmar, 1976. 20p. ISBN Unavailable. $3. Gr.
1-3.
     A beetle embarks on a heart-warming search for his
lost light. All his friends try to help him: a bird suggests an electric battery, a pigeon tries carrying him, a

snake proposes lighting matches, a magpie gives him a mir-
ror, and finally the sun gives him a piece of sunlight that
penetrates his body forever. Handsome illustrations complement this delightful animal story.

Hefter, Richard. Una blanca sonrisa de cocodrilo: el libro
de los números [Crocodile's White Smile: Book of Numbers].
Translated by Concepción Zendrera. Barcelona: Editorial
Juventud S.A., 1980. 30p. ISBN 84-261-1686-8. $3.50.
Gr. PK-2.
Bright, colorful illustrations and a simple text introduce
children to numbers one through 10.

_____. Colores [Colors]. ISBN 84-261-1982-4.

_____. Mirar [To Look]. ISBN 84-261-1980-8.

_____. Las palabras [Words]. ISBN 84-261-1984-0.

Ea. vol.: Translated by Enric Monforte. 30p. (El
libro de la fresa). Barcelona: Editorial Juventud, 1983.
$3. Gr. K-2.
In characteristic Hefter style, these three easy-to-read
books depict colors, simple concepts in a day of shopping
with bear family, and simple words about things on the
farm, at the circus, on the street, at home, and other lo-
cations. Bold, colorful illustrations and a simple text
make these books appealing to beginning Spanish readers.

Hill, Eric. El cumpleaños de Spot [Spot's Birthday]. New
York: G. P. Putnam's Sons, 1982. [24p.] ISBN 0-399-
21020-2. $9.95. Gr. PK-2.
Spot plays hide-and-seek with his friends at his birthday party. Simple text and illustrations guide young readers to lift especially designed flaps which, when opened,
show where his friends are hiding.

Hill, Eric. ¿Dónde está Spot? [Where Is Spot?]. New York:
G. P. Putnam's Sons, 1980. [20p.] ISBN Unavailable.
$8.95. Gr. PK-2.
Spot, a young puppy, is nowhere to be found. His

mother looks for him in a closet, inside a clock, inside a
piano, under a stairway, under a bed, under a carpet,
until a little turtle tells her where Spot can be found.
The simple Spanish text and illustrations, as well as the
especially designed flaps which young readers must open
to read all of the story, add interest and fun to the story.

Hill, Eric. El primer paseo de Spot [Spot's First Walk]. New
York: G. P. Putnam's Sons, 1981. [22p.] ISBN 0-399-
21019-9. $9.95. Gr. PK-2.
    Spot's exciting first walk includes encounters with an
angry cat and with a mother hen and her baby chicks:
looking at a woodpecker tapping a hole in a tree; finding
fresh flowers, a carrot, and a bone; and returning home
exhausted. The simple Spanish text and illustrations, as
well as the especially designed flaps which young readers
must open to read all of the story, are fun.

Hill, Eric. La primera navidad de Spot [Spot's First Christ-
mas]. New York: G. P. Putnam's Sons, 1983. 24p.
ISBN 0-399-21024-5. $9.95. Gr. PK-2.
    Spot's preparations for his first Christmas include wrap-
ping gifts, decorating the Christmas tree, listening to
Christmas carols, and opening his gift. The simple Spanish text and illustrations, as well as the especially designed flaps which young readers must open to read all
of the story, are indeed fun.

Hill, Eric. Spot va a la escuela [Spot Goes to School]. ISBN
0-399-21223-X.

_____. Spot va a la playa [Spot Goes to the Beach]. ISBN
0-399-21259-0.

    Ea. vol.: [22p.] Color illustrations. (Libros de Spot).
New York: G. P. Putnam's Sons, 1984. $9.95. Gr. PK-
2.
    Like previous Spot books, these include simple texts in
Spanish, colorful illustrations, and the especially designed
flaps which children must open to read all of the story.
Spot va a la escuela shows Spot's first day at school: He
is greeted by his teacher and new friends, singing songs,

playing with blocks, showing his bone, playing outdoors,
listening to a story, painting pictures, and delighted about
his new experiences. Spot va a la playa shows Spot enjoying a day at the beach with his parents. He gets a
new hat, plays ball with his father, builds sand castles,
goes fishing, falls into the ocean, finds a new girlfriend,
and returns home. These are indeed fun books for young
readers.

Hoff, Syd.   Danielito y el dinosauro [Danny and the Dino-
saur]. Illustrated by the author. Translated by Pura
Belpré. New York: Harper and Row Publishers, 1969.
64p. ISBN 0-06-022469-X. $9.89. Gr. 1-3.
     The charming story Danny and the Dinosaur is avail-
able in Spanish and will certainly please all Spanish young
readers. Danny's newly-found pet and their exciting day
in the city, at the zoo, at the park, and with Danny's
friends will amuse and delight all boys and girls.
     The alluring illustrations and simplicity of the language
make this book especially recommended for young Spanish
readers.

Kessler, Leonard. Aquí viene el ponchado [Here Comes the
Strikeout]. Translated by Pura Belpré. New York:
Harper and Row Publishers, 1969. 64p. ISBN 0-06-
023154-8. $9.89. Gr. 2-4.
     Originally published in English under the title Here
Comes the Strikeout, this Spanish version has maintained
the fast pace and interest of its predecessor. Robertito
("Little Robert") could not get a hit; he had gone to bat
20 times and he had struck out. His friend Guillermito
offered to help. They practiced and practiced until
Robertito finally learned how to hit. So, when Robertito's
team played an important game, Robertito got a hit, and
his time won the game.
     Baseball lovers will enjoy this well-written story with
simple illustrations.

Lacau, María Hortensia. El pollito pícaro y consentido [The
Spoiled and Naughty Chick]. Illustrated by Cristina
Ramos de Siri. Buenos Aires: Editorial Plus Ultra, 1981.
[26p.] ISBN Unavailable. $3. Gr. 1-3.

150   Basic Collection of Books in Spanish

Appealing story about a naughty chick who was warned
by his mother/hen and father/rooster not to sing on a
fence or else he could be eaten by a falcon. He ignored
his parents' warnings and was scared to death by a falcon
and saved by his parents.
The simple text and cheerful illustrations add interest
to this story.

Llega un hermanito [A Little Brother Arrives]. Buenos Aires:
Editorial Sigmar, 1974. 6p. ISBN Unavailable. $3. Gr.
K-3.
Short, attractive story with pleasing illustrations of a
little girl and her feelings upon the arrival of a baby
brother. The simple vocabulary shows Mama pregnant,
nursing baby, dressing the nude baby boy, and, finally,
the little girl enjoying the undivided attention of Papa
and Mama when baby sleeps.

Lobel, Arnold. El buho en su casa [An Owl at Home].
Translated by Pablo Lizcano. Madrid: Ediciones Alfaguara, 1982. 66p. ISBN 84-204-3063-3. $4.50. Gr. 2-
4.
An owl at home experiences many things, such as an
uninvited guest, strange objects in bed, tea made out of
tears, going up and down the stairs, and a special friend,
the moon. Charming illustrations and a good translation
make this a fun book for young readers.

Mayne, William. La gata de retales [The Patchwork Cat].
Illustrated by Nicola Bayley. Translated by Humpty Dumpty. Barcelona: Editorial Lumen, 1983. [32p.] ISBN 84-
264-3581-5. $6. Gr. 2-4.
Taby, the cat, loved to play, sleep, and eat with her
old patchwork blanket. One day, the lady of the house
threw away the blanket because it was getting very dirty
and, besides, she was going to buy a basket for Taby.
Taby did not want a basket; she wanted her old blanket.
Thus Taby goes out in search of her beloved blanket.
Taby's experiences have a happy ending when she finally
finds her blanket and returns home where she can now keep
her blanket--after mother has washed it. Pastel illustrations of Taby in various predicaments accompany the lively
text.

Oxenbury, Helen. En casa de los abuelos [At Grandparent's
House]. ISBN 84-261-2065-2.

_____. Nuestro perro [Our Dog]. ISBN 84-261-2066-0.

_____. La visita [The Visitor]. ISBN 84-261-2067-9.

    Ea. vol.: [18p.] Translated by Concepción Zendrera.
(Los Libros del Chiquitín). Barcelona: Editorial Juventud,
1984. $5. Gr. K-2.
    Charming pastel illustrations and easy-to-read texts
describe happy moments in the life of children. En casa
de lost abuelos tells about a little girl's weekly visits to her
grandparents' house. Some readers may object to some
stereotypical views of older people, such as grandmother
knitting and wearing house slippers, and grandfather not
being able to crawl out from under a table. This is, nonetheless, a warm story about a little girl and her grandparents. Nuestro perro shows what happens when a little
boy and his mother take their dog out for a walk. La
visita describes the day mother had an important visitor
at home with embarrassing consequences.

Perera, Hilda. Rana ranita [Little Frog]. Illustrated by A.
Anievas. Madrid: Editorial Everest, S.A., 1981. [32p.]
ISBN 84-241-5261-1. $4. Gr. 2-4.
    Amusing story about a little frog that wanted to be-
come a blue jay. She befriended a blue jay who promised
to teach her how to become a blue jay. After many unsuccessful attempts, the little frog decided to marry a toad
and to be a frog forever. Colorful illustrations complement the humorous text.

Potter, Beatrix. Pedrín, el conejo travieso [The Tale of
Peter Rabbit]. New York: Frederick Warne, 1985. 59p.
ISBN 07232-1797-1. $4.50. Gr. 2-4.
    Tiny pastel illustrations beautifully complement this
well-done translation of The Tale of Peter Rabbit. The
small size (4¼" x 5½"), unfortunately, makes it difficult to
use for reading aloud to children. Individual children,
however, will delight in Peter's amusing misadventures.

Rey, H. A. Jorge el curioso [Curious George]. Translated
by Pedro Villa Fernandez. Boston: Houghton Mifflin Co.,
1961. 57p. ISBN 0-395-24909-0. $7.95. Gr. 2-4.
    Curious George, originally published in 1941, is still a
favorite of many young readers. This Spanish translation
engages the reader with the witticism of "Jorge el curioso,"
the curious monkey who constantly gets in trouble and finally ends up in the zoo.
    It includes a vocabulary of Spanish words translated in-
to English at the end of the book as well as translations
of Spanish phrases and expressions at the foot of each
page.

Rico, Lolo, and Cruz Blanco. Kalamito tiene una hermanita
[Kalamito Has a Little Sister]. Illustrated by Irene Bor-
doy. Madrid: Ediciones Altea, 1982. [24p.] ISBN 84-
372-1630-3. $4. Gr. 2-4.
    The feelings of little possum-like Kalamito, who just had
a baby sister, are genuinely depicted in this down-to-
earth story with attractive illustration. Kalamito expresses
honest anger, jealousy, and resentment because his mother
now devotes more time and attention to his ugly, newborn
sister. He finally realizes that it isn't all that bad to
have a new sister.

Sendak, Maurice. Donde viven los monstruos [Where the Wild
Things Are]. Illustrated by the author. Translated by
Agustín Gervás. Madrid: Ediciones Alfaguara, 1984.
[38p.] ISBN 84-204-3022-6. $15. Gr. K-2.
    Sendak's award-winning Where the Wild Things Are has
been delightfully translated for the Spanish-speaking reader. Young readers will enjoy Max's dream of going where
the wild things are, ruling them, sharing their rumpus and,
finally, returning home where someone loves him.

Stinson, Kathy. El rojo es el mejor [Red Is Best]. Illus-
trated by Robin Baird Lewis. Translated by Kiki and
Clarisa de la Rosa. Caracas: Ediciones Ekaré-Banco del
Libro, 1958. [28p.] ISBN 84-8351-034-0. $6.50. Gr.
PK-2.
    Isabella, a little girl, tells why she thinks the color red
is best: She can jump higher with her red stockings. She

feels like Little Red Riding Hood with her red jacket. She
can walk better with her red slippers. Orange juice tastes
better in her red glass. And she looks beautiful with her
red bows. Engaging, three-tone line illustrations show
Isabella delighted with the color red. Young children will
be charmed by Isabella's reasoning.

Stinson, Kathy. Soy grande, soy pequeño [Big or Little].
Illustrated by Robin Baird Lewis. Translated by Kiki and
Clarisa de la Rosa. Caracas: Ediciones Ekaré-Banco del
Libro, 1985. [28p.] ISBN 84-8351-035-9. $6.50. Gr.
PK-2.
A little boy tells that at times he feels like a big boy
and others like a little boy. For example, he feels like a
big boy when he can get dressed by himself, when he
remembers to take a book to school, when he can prepare
his own breakfast, and when he talks with his father about
spaceships. He feels like a little boy when his bed is wet
in the morning, when his mother punishes him, when he
gets lost at the grocery store, and when he falls asleep in
front of the television set and papa must carry him to bed.
Alluring pastel illustrations complement this story about a
boy's honest feelings.

Ugalde Alcántara, Felipe. Los números [Numbers]. México:
Editorial Patria, 1984. [20p.] ISBN 968-39-0090-9. $3.50.
Gr. Pre-School-2.
Striking watercolor illustrations introduce children to
numbers one through ten. Most of the illustrations include
Mexican motifs, making this simple counting book of special
interest to Hispanic children.

Ungerer, Tomi. Adelaide [Adelaide]. Illustrated by the author. Translated by Pablo Lizcano. Madrid: Ediciones
Alfaguara, 1983. 44p. ISBN 84-204-3704-2. $3.50. Gr.
1-3.
Well-done translation of T. Ungerer's Adelaide, the
charming story of a courageous, flying kangaroo who visits
many countries, gets in trouble in some, but ends a real
heroine by saving two children from a building on fire.
Her subsequent encounter with another kangaroo gives this
story a happy ending. The original, witty line illustrations
complement the story.

Ungerer, Tomi. Emil [Emil]. Translated by Pablo Lizcano.
Madrid: Ediciones Alfaguara, 1983. 35p. ISBN 84-204-
3705-0. $3.50. Gr. 2-4.
The delightful adventures of Emil, the courageous octopus, are now available in this well-done translation for
young Spanish readers. Witty, three-tone illustrations accompany the engaging story about a simple octopus who
became a town's hero.

Ungerer, Tomi. Rufus [Rufus]. Translated by Pablo Lizcano.
Madrid: Ediciones Alfaguara, 1983. [34p.] ISBN 84-204-
3706-9. $3.50. Gr. 2-4.
Rufus, the playful bat, decided to see the world during
daytime. He painted himself with bright colors and started
to fly. Some people got scared and shot him. Fortunately,
a famous doctor took him home and cared for him. After
a while, Rufus got homesick, but he and the doctor remained friends. This is a good translation with the original, striking illustrations.

Vannini, Marisa. Los cuatro gatitos [The Four Kittens]. Illustrated by Paula Acarin. Barcelona: Editorial Juventud,
1983. [28p.] ISBN 84-261-1792-9. $3. Gr. 1-3.
Once upon a time there were four kittens: a black kitten, a white kitten, a brown kitten, and a hairless kitten.
They were brothers and cared very much for each other.
Hairless kitten was quite unattractive but his brothers
made sure nobody made fun of him. So, when they went
to school for the first time and a big, bully cat started
making fun of hairless kitten, all the brothers immediately
came to his rescue and hairless kitten was never bothered
in school again. Colorful, bold illustrations of kittens and
cats in various situations complement the entertaining text.

Vigna, Judith. Gregorio y sus puntos [Gregory's Stitches].
Illustrated by the author. Translated by Alma Flor Ada.
Chicago: Albert Whitman & Co., 1976. [32p.] ISBN 0-
8075-3044-1. $9.25. Gr. 2-4.
This Spanish version of Gregory's Stitches has maintained the fast pace of the original. It tells how each one
of Gregory's friends changes the story of how he got six
stitches in his forehead. He was thus declared "a real

hero" and "getting stitches didn't seem so terrible after
all." Clever illustrations complement the easy-to-read
text.

Vincent, Gabrielle. César y Ernestina han perdido a Gedeón
[Cesar and Ernestina Lose Gedeón]. Barcelona: Editorial
Timun Mas, S.A., 1982? [26p.] ISBN 84-7176-448-2.
$3.50. Gr. 2-4.
    Ernestina, a small rat, loses her favorite stuffed animal,
a penguin. César, a big bear, tries to comfort her but
she is heartbroken. Thus César decides to make a new
stuffed animal for her. They celebrate the return of
Gedeón, the penguin, with a big party. Alluring pastel
illustrations complement the simple text.

Vincent, Gabrielle. César y Ernestina músicos callejeros
[Cesar and Ernestina Street Musicians]. Barcelona:
Editorial Timun Mas, S.A., 1982? [26p.] ISBN 84-7176-
447-4. $3.50. Gr. 2-4.
    César, a big bear, and Ernestina, a small rat, need
money to fix the roof of their house. Thus, they decide
to become street musicians; César plays the violin and
Ernestina sings beautiful songs. They make a lot of
money and go on a shopping spree. The simple illustrations and text will appeal to young readers.

Vincent, Gabrielle. César y Ernestina van al fotógrafo [Ce-
sar and Ernestina Go to a Photographer]. Barcelona:
Editorial Timun Mas, S.A., 1982? 26p. ISBN 84-7176-
304-6. $3.50. Gr. 2-4.
    César, a big bear, and Ernestina, a small rat, have a
misunderstanding regarding some photographs. Ernestina
feels sad and rejected because she does not appear on any
of César's pictures. César offers a solution; they go to
a photographer to have their pictures taken. Simple text
and ingenuous illustrations make this story fun to read.

Vincent, Gabrielle. César y Ernestina van de picnic [Cesar
and Ernestina Go on a Picnic]. Barcelona: Editorial
Timun Mas, S.A., 1982? 26p. ISBN 84-7176-303-7. $3.50
Gr. 2-4.

Through brief dialogues between César, a big bear, and Ernestina, a small rat, and witty pastel illustrations, young readers participate in a marvelous outdoor picnic in a rainstorm. What appeared to be an unfortunate rainy day at home, turned out to be a most enjoyable day in the country with new friends at a magnificent mansion.

Wylie, Joanne and David. Un cuento curioso de colores [A Fishy Color Story]. ISBN 0-516-32983-9.

_____, and _____. Un cuento de un pez grande [A Big Fish Story]. ISBN 0-516-32982-0.

Ea. vol.: 28p. Illustrated by the authors. Translated by Lada Kratky. (Los Cuentos Curiosos de Peces). Chicago: Children's Press, 1984. $8.25. Gr. K-2.
Abstract, colorful illustrations and simple questions and answers in Spanish characterize this excellent translation of the series, "Fishy Fish Stories." Un cuento curioso de colores introduces the colors through a child's story about a fish. Un cuento de un pez grande describes the size of a fish through words that keep increasing in size. A Spanish word list at the end of each book makes these stories useful as vocabulary building as well as simple entertainment.

Zuliani, Fausto, La bolita azul [The Little Blue Ball]. Illustrated by Gustavo Bech. Buenos Aires: Editorial Plus Ultra, 1981. [26p.] ISBN Unavailable. $3. Gr. 2-4.
Diego lost his little blue ball. He looked and looked but couldn't find it. He asked a little bird; he asked an airplane; he asked a seller of candy; nobody has seen his little blue ball. He started to cry when suddenly the guard at the park told him where his little blue ball was.
This is a fast-paced story that will delight children. The unsophisticated illustrations add a special charm too.

Zuliani, Fausto. Don Escarabajo tiene un color [Mr. Black Beetle Has One Color]. Illustrated by Laura Thorkelsen. Buenos Aires: Editorial Plus Ultra, 1981. [26p.] ISBN Unavailable. $3. Gr. 3-5.
Yellow Rose, Red Rose, and White Daisy are very sad;

they wished to be adorned with other colors. Black beetle
comes along and has enough paint to paint only one of them.
They all give their reasons for wishing to be painted, but
White Daisy was the most convincing: She was never vis-
ited by any butterfly because of her extreme whiteness.
So Black beetle painted her heart a beautiful golden color.
Red Rose and Yellow Rose were so angry that since that
moment they have been covered with thorns.

Simple, charming illustrations complement this story of
jealous and sad flowers.

- SECTION VI: PROFESSIONAL BOOKS

Prof 010 BIBLIOGRAPHY INCLUDING BIBLIOGRAPHIES OF
READING FOR CHILDREN AND YOUNG ADULTS

Dale, Doris Cruger. Bilingual Books in Spanish and English
for Children. Littleton, Colo.: Libraries Unlimited, 1985.
163p. ISBN 0-87287-477-X. $23.50. Gr. Adults.
    The author identifies and evaluates 254 bilingual books
in Spanish and English for children published or distributed
in the United States since 1940. It must be noted that her
main purpose was to produce a historical record of the publication of bilingual books, rather than to produce an ac-
quisition guide for in-print books. This is an informative
guide for those interested in locating reviewing sources of
bilingual materials in the U.S.

Duran, Daniel Flores. Latino Materials: A Multimedia Guide
for Children and Young Adults. Santa Barbara, Calif.:
ABC-Clio Press, 1979. 249p. ISBN 0-87436-262-8. $22.95.
Gr. Adults.
    Selection guide of books and films for elementary and
secondary schools that includes 286 titles about Mexican
Americans, 126 titles about Puerto Ricans, and 61 general
reference items. Materials in English, Spanish, and bilingual formats are included. It does not include materials
about Cuba or South America.

Libros en Español: An Annotated List of Children's Books in
Spanish. New York: New York Public Library, 1978.
52p. ISBN 0-87104-628-8. $2.50. Gr. Adults.
    Picture books, books in Spanish for children, bilingual
books, books for learning Spanish, and recordings are
briefly annotated in this list.

Schon·, Isabel.   Books in Spanish for Children and Young
     Adults: An Annotated Guide.   Metuchen, N.J.:   Scare-
     crow Press, 1978.   165p.   ISBN 0-8108-1176-6. $15.   Gr.
     Adults.
     This is a guide to books in Spanish for children of pre-
school through high-school age from 13 Spanish-speaking
countries.   Most of the books included cover the period
1973-1978.   Annotations (in English) are descriptive and
evaluative, with designations of outstanding, marginal, or
not recommended.   It also includes tentative grade level
assignments.

_____.   Books in Spanish for Children and Young Adults:
     An Annotated Guide, Series II.   Metuchen, N.J.:   Scare-
     crow Press, 1983.   174p.   ISBN 0-8108-1620-2. $15.   Gr.
     Adults.
     Like its predecessor, this is a guide to books in Span-
ish for children of preschool through high-school age from
11 Spanish-speaking countries.   Most of the books included
cover the period 1978-1982.

_____.   Books in Spanish for Children and Young Adults:
     An Annotated Guide, Series III.   Metuchen, N.J.:   Scare-
     crow Press, 1985.   208p.   ISBN 0-8108-1807-8. $16.50.
     Gr. Adults.
     Like its predecessors, this is a guide to books in Span-
ish for children and young adults from 12 Spanish-speaking
countries and the U.S.   Most of the books included cover
the period 1982-1984.   Annotations (in English) are descriptive and evaluative, with designations of outstanding,
marginal, or not recommended.   Appendices provide names
and addresses of reliable book dealers in Spanish-speaking
countries and book dealers in the U.S. who specialize in
books in Spanish.

               Prof 015.72 BIBLIOGRAPHIES OF WORKS
                          FROM MEXICO

Schon, Isabel.   Mexico and Its Literature for Children and
     Adolescents.   Tempe, Ariz.:   Center for Latin American
     Studies, Arizona State University, 1977.   54p.   ISBN 0-
     87918-033-1. $3.   Gr. Adults.

This is a study of the literature for children and adolescents of Mexico. It discusses the economic and educational problems of Mexico as well as the Mexican authors of
the nineteenth and twentieth centuries.

Prof 809 HISTORY, DESCRIPTION, CRITICAL DESCRIPTION
OF MORE THAN ONE LITERATURE

Bravo-Villasante, Carmen. Literatura infantil universal [Uni-
versal Children's Literature]. Illustrated by Manuel Boix.
Madrid: Almena, 1978. 2 volumes. 325p.; 305p. ISBN
84-7014-019-1. $41. Gr. Adult.
This is a succinct overview of the history and bibliography of the literature for children of many countries
with outstanding illustrations.

Prof 860 LITERATURES OF SPANISH AND
PORTUGUESE LANGUAGES

Bravo-Villasante, Carmen. Antología de la literatura infantil
española [Anthology of Spanish Children's Literature]. Illustrated by Celedonio Perellón and Adan Ferrer. 6th
Edition. Madrid: Editorial Doncel, 1983. 2 volumes.
392p.; 394p. ISBN 84-325-0392-4. $21. Gr. Adult.
The purpose of this anthology is to introduce the best
Spanish authors who have written for children. Historical in scope, it includes brief biographical notes and ex-
cerpts from the works of Spanish authors from the thir-
teenth century up to 1949. This 6th edition has a new
section on folklore.

_____. Historia de la literatura infantil española [History
of Spanish Children's Literature]. Illustrations: Reprints
from Isopete historiado (Zaragoza, 1489) and Exemplario
contra los engaños y peligros del mundo (1493). 4th ed.
Madrid: Editorial Doncel, 1983. 339p. ISBN 84-325-
0391-6. $12. Gr. Adult.
The history of children's literature in Spanish from the
Middle Ages to the present is examined by the well-known
Spanish author Bravo-Villasante. This is a most complete
resource for the study of Spanish children's literature.

_____. Historia y antología de la literatura infantil ibero-
americana [History and Anthology of Latin American Children's Literature]. 2nd ed. Madrid: Editorial Doncel,
1982. 2 volumes. 467p.; 442p. ISBN 84-325-0386-X.
$28. Gr. Adult.
  These two volumes include a brief history and an anthology of children's literature from Latin America, Portu-
gal, and the Philippines.

- APPENDIX: DEALERS OF BOOKS IN SPANISH

ARGENTINA

Fernando García Cambeiro
Cochabamba 244
1150 Buenos Aires, Argentina

CHILE

Herta Berenguer L.
Publicaciones
Correo 9, Casilla 16598
Santiago, Chile

COLOMBIA

Libros de Colombia y Latinoamérica
Transversal 39 No. 124-30
Barrio El Batán
Bogotá, Colombia

COSTA RICA

Librería Lehmann, S.A.
Apdo. 10011
San José, Costa Rica

CUBA

Ediciones Vitral, Inc.
G.P.O. Box 1913
New York, NY 10116

ECUADOR

Sr. Jaime Jeremias
Libri Mundi
Juan Leon Mera, 851
Quito, Ecuador

MEXICO

Haydea Conde
Avenida Toluca #811-casa 14
Col. Olivar de los Padres
Del. A. Obregón
México 01780, D.F. México

PERU

E. Iturriaga and Cia, S.A.
Casilla 4640
Lima, Peru

PUERTO RICO

Thekes, Inc.
Plaza de las Américas
Hato Rey, Puerto Rico   00918

SPAIN

Libros Talentum
Nuñez de Balboa, 53
Madrid 1, España

UNITED STATES

Baker & Taylor
Books in Spanish
380 Edison Way
Reno, NV   89564

Bilingual Publications Co.
1966 Broadway
New York, NY   10023

French and Spanish Book Corp.
652 Olive Street
Los Angeles, CA   90014

French and Spanish Book Corp.
115 Fifth Avenue
New York, NY   10003

Hispanic Books Distributors
240 E. Yvon Drive
Tucson, AZ   85704

Iaconi Book Imports
300 Pennsylvania Avenue
San Francisco, CA   94107

Lectorum Publications, Inc.
137 West 14th Street
New York, NY   10011

Pan American Book Co.
4326 Melrose Avenue
Los Angeles, CA   90029

URUGUAY

Barreiro y Ramos, S.A.
25 de Mayo 604
Casilla de Correo 15
Montevideo, Uruguay

VENEZUELA

Soberbia Cia
Edificio Dillon-Local 4 Este 2, no. 139
Puente Yanes a Tracabordo
Caracas 1010, Venezuela

- AUTHOR INDEX

- TITLE INDEX

171

- SUBJECT INDEX

ACCIDENTS--FICTION
Vigna, Judith: Gregorio y sus puntos 154

AFRICA
Los animales de Africa 43
Los animales de la sabana africana 43
Los animales de la selva y estepa africana 43
Los animales de los ríos y los lagos de Africa 43

AFRICA--FICTION
Hemingway, Ernest: El buen león 114
Paz, Marcela: Papelucho misionero 122

AGRICULTURE
La agricultura 54, 96
Echeverría, Eugenia: Las frutas 55
Giron, Nicole: El azúcar 55, 93
Noriega, Luisa de: Yo soy el durazno 55
Puncel, María: Cuando sea mayor trabajaré en una granja 54
Vallarta, Luz del Carmen: El chocolate 55

AIR
Peñarroja, Jordi: Juega con ... el aire 32

AIRPLANES
Chant, Chris: El reactor comercial desde el despeque hasta el
    aterrizaje 53, 87
Usborne, Peter, and Su Swallow: Aviones 53, 85

AIRPLANES--HISTORY
Segrelles, Vicente: Historia ilustrada de la aviación desde los
    inicios hasta 1935 48

ALLIGATORS see CROCODILES

ALLIGATORS--FICTION
Puncel, María: Clara y el caimán 124

ALMANACS
Almanaque mundial 1986 1
Guinness libro de los records 1

AMAZON
   Los animales de la selva amazónica 43

AMERICA
   Los animales de la pradera americana 43

AMPHIBIANS
   Kincaid, Lucy: Mira abajo 31

AMUSEMENT PARKS--FICTION
   Delgado, Eduardo: Mientras Tim juega en el parque de atracciones
      143

ANGER
   Simon, Norma: Cuando me enojo 9

ANGER--FICTION
   Balzola, Asun: Munia y el cocolilo naranja 132

ANIMALS (see also specific terms: e.g., DOGS, CATS, PETS)
   Los animales de Africa 43
   Los animales de América del Norte 43
   Los animales de América del Sur 43
   Los animales de Asia 43
   Los animales de la casa y del jardín 42
   Los animales de la jungla, estepas y montañas de Asia y Oceanía
      43
   Los animales de la montaña y el valle 43
   Los animales de la playa y de la costa 43
   Los animales de la pradera americana 43
   Los animales de la prehistoria 43
   Los animales de la sabana africana 43
   Los animales de la selva amazónica 43
   Los animales de la selva y estepa africana 43
   Los animales de la tundra y de los hielos 43
   Los animales de los llanos y montañas de Europa 44
   Los animales de los ríos y los lagos de Africa 43
   Los animales de Oceanía 43
   Los animales del bosque y del monte 42
   Los animales del lago y del pantano 43
   Los animales del mar y de las lagunas 43
   Los animales del océano y de los abismos 43
   Los animales del río y del estanque 42
   Los animales marinos 44
   Armellada de Aspe, Virginia: La lana 56
   Las aves 46, 96
   Bonnardel, Rene: Lionel y los animales de la montaña 78, 98
   Clark, Mary Lou: Dinosaurios 39, 84
   Ferrán, Jaime: Mañana de parque 42
   García Sánchez, José Luis, and Miguel Angel Pacheco: El coco-
      drilo 46

ANIMALS (cont.)

ANIMALS--FICTION

192 Basic Collection of Books in Spanish

BIOGRAPHY
  Alavedra, José: La extraordinaria vida de Pablo Casals 82
  García Barquero, Juan Antonio: Juan Sebastián Bach 83
  Morán, Francisco José: Leonardo Da Vinci 83
  Morán, Francisco José: Pablo Ruiz Picasso 83

BIOLOGY
  Dos cuentos de vida 39
  Schkolnick, Saul: Colorín colorado, ovulito fecundado 39

BIRDS (see also specific birds: e.g., CHICKENS, EAGLES)
  Las aves 46, 96
  Dos cuentos de vida 39
  Herring, Philippine, and Fetze Pijlman: Como vive un ave acuática:
    el somormujo 46
  Kincaid, Lucy: Mira arriba 32

BIRDS--FICTION
  Lobel, Arnold: El buho en su casa 150
  Posadas Mañé, Carmen de: Kiwi 123

BIRTH see REPRODUCTION

BIRTHDAYS--FICTION
  Hill, Eric: El cumpleaños de Spot 147

BOARDING SCHOOLS--FICTION
  Paz, Marcela: Papelucho 120

BOATS see SHIPS AND SAILING

BOATS--FICTION
  Gorostiza, Carlos: El barquito viajero 146

BOOKS AND READING
  Dale, Doris Cruger: Bilingual Books in Spanish and English for
    Children 158
  Duran, Daniel Flores: Latino materials: A multimedia guide for
    children and young adults 158
  Libros en Español: An Annotated List of Children's Books in
    Spanish 158
  Schon, Isabel: Books in Spanish for Children and Young Adults:
    an annotated guide 159
  Schon, Isabel: Books in Spanish for Children and Young Adults:
    an annotated guide, series II 159
  Schon, Isabel: Books in Spanish for Children and Young Adults:
    an annotated guide, series III 159
  Schon, Isabel: Mexico and Its Literature for Children and
    Adolescents 159

BOYS--FICTION (cont.)

BOYS--FICTION (cont.)

CAREER EDUCATION

CASALS, PABLO

CASSETTES

CATS

CATS--FICTION

CAVES--FICTION
Company, Mercé: Perdidos en la cueva 109

CERAMICS
La cerámica 60, 96
Giron, Nicole: El barro 60

CHEATING--FICTION
Lööf, Jan: Historia de una manzana roja 118

CHEMISTRY
Peñarroja, Jordi: Juega con ... la química 32

CHICKENS--FICTION
Friskey, Margaret: Pollito Pequeñito cuenta hasta diez 146
Lacau, María Hortensia: El pollito pícaro y consentido 149

CHILDREN see BOYS, GIRLS, BABIES

CHILDREN--FICTION
Sánchez, J. L. Ga., and Pacheco, M. A.: Los niños que no
tenían escuelas 125

CHILDREN'S LITERATURE see LITERATURE--CHILDREN

CHILE--FICTION
Paz, Marcela: Papelucho 120
Paz, Marcela: Papelucho casi huérfano 120
Paz, Marcela: Papelucho detective 121
Paz, Marcela: Papelucho: diario secreto de Papelucho y el mar-
ciano 121
Paz, Marcela: Papelucho en vacaciones 121
Paz, Marcela: Papelucho historiador 122
Paz, Marcela: Papelucho: mi hermana Ji 122
Paz, Marcela: Papelucho: mi hermano Hippie 122
Paz, Marcela: Papelucho perdido 123

CHRISTMAS see HOLIDAYS

CHRISTMAS--FICTION
Capdevila, Juan: Teo y su familia 138
Chapouton, Anne-Marie: Los Bambalinos celebran la Navidad 138
Denou, Violeta: Es navidad, Teo 143
Hill, Eric: La primera navidad de Spot 148

CHRISTMAS--POETRY
Cichello, Rubén D. and Clara Inés Fernández: Papa Noel y la
historia de navidad 9

EL CID
Gefaell, María Luisa: El Cid 73
Aguirre Bellver, Joaquín: El juglar del Cid 101

CIRCUSES
   Ferrán, Jaime: Tarde de circo 63
   García Sánchez, José Luis: El circo 1 64
   García Sánchez, José Luis: El circo 2 64
   García Sánchez, José Luis: El circo 3 64

CIRCUSES--FICTION
   Capdevila, Juan: Teo en el circo 137

CITY LIFE--FICTION
   Aboites, Luis: El campo y la ciudad 101
   Amo, Montserrat Del: Aparecen los "Blok" 102
   Belgrano, Margarita: Los zapatos voladores 104
   Escofet, Christian: Llueve en la ciudad 145
   Sánchez, J. L. Ga., and Pacheco, M. A.: Los niños que no
      tenían escuelas 125
   Solano Flores, Guillermo: La calle 11, 99

CLIMATOLOGY
   Ford, Adam: Observando el clima 38, 94

COLORS--FICTION
   Amarillo girasol 131
   Azul marino 131
   Azul rey 131
   Blanco aparicio 131
   Hefter, Richard: Colores 147
   Marrón ratón 131
   Negra escobilla 131
   Púrpura candido 131
   Roja sorpresa 131
   Roso ronquillo 131
   Stinson, Kathy: El rojo es el mejor 152
   Verde gruñón 132
   Wylie, Joanne and David: Un cuento curioso de colores 156
   Zuliani, Fausto: Don Escarabajo tiene un color 156

COMPOSERS
   García Barquero, Juan Antonio: Juan Sebastián Bach 83

COMPUTER LANGUAGES
   Smith, Brian Reffin: Programación de computadoras 8, 92
   Watt, Sofía, and Miguel Mangada: Basic para Niños 8

COMPUTER PROGRAMMING see PROGRAMMING (ELECTRONIC
   COMPUTERS)

COMPUTERS
   Bramhill, Peter: El mundo de la computadora 7
   Graham, Ian: Juegos de computadoras 65, 92
   Graham, Ian: El ordenador 7, 87

ELEPHANTS--FICTION
  Ballesta, Juan: Tommy y el elefante 104
  Osorio, Marta: El último elefante blanco 68

EMOTIONS
  Simon, Norma: Cuando me enojo 9

EMPLOYMENT see OCCUPATIONS, WORK, CAREER EDUCATION

ENCYCLOPEDIAS--DICTIONARIES
  A Child's Picture Dictionary English/Spanish 3
  Diccionario enciclopédico Espasa 1
  Diccionario Temático: Simónimos y Antónimos 4
  Enciclopedia Barsa 1
  Godman, Arthur: Diccionario ilustrado de las ciencias 5
  González, Mike: Collins Concise Spanish-English English-Spanish
    Dictionary 4
  Javier, Carlos, and Taranilla de la Varga: Diccionario temático
    de historia del arte 5
  Loippe, Ulla: Lo que los niños quieren saber 2
  McNaught, Harry: 500 palabras nuevas para ti 31
  Manley, Deborah: Es divertido descubrir cosas 2
  Mi primer Sopena: diccionario infantil ilustrado 4
  Montes, Graciela: Gran enciclopedia de los pequeños 45
  El niño pregunta: Los animales del zoo; los árboles 3
  El niño pregunta: Las carreras de coches; la fuerza de la
    naturaleza 3
  Sopena Inglés de los niños: diccionario infantil ilustrado, Español-
    Inglés 4
  Zendrera, Concepción and Noelle Granger: Mi primer diccionario
    ilustrado 5

ENERGY
  Satchwell, John: Como funciona la energía 52, 94

ENGLISH LANGUAGE--DICIONARIES
  A Child's picture dictionary English/Spanish 3
  González, Mike: Collins Concise Spanish-English English-Spanish
    Dictionary 4
  McNaught, Harry: 500 palabras nuevas para ti 31
  Sopena Inglés de los niños; diccionario infantil ilustrado, Español-
    Inglés 4

EUROPE
  Los animales de los llanos y montañas de Europa 44
  Anno, Mitsumasa: El viaje de Anno I--Europa del Norte 80

EXERCISES--FICTION
  Charles, Donald: El libro de ejercicios de Gato Galano 139

EXPERIMENTS
  Cobb, Vicki: Experimentos científicos que se pueden comer 33

FAMILY LIFE (cont.)
     D'Atri, Adriana: Así pasamos el día   141
     D'Atri, Adriana: Así somos nosotros   141

FANTASY (see also FABLES, FAIRY TALES, SCIENCE FICTION)
     Carroll, Lewis: "Alicia" para los niños   89, 106
     Chapouton, Anne-Marie: Los Bambalinos celebran la Navidad   138
     Chapouton, Anne-Marie: Los Bambalinos y el elixir de sol   138
     Chapouton, Anne-Marie: Los Bambalinos y las ranas   138
     Turin, Adela: Las cajas de cristal   126

FARMS
     La agricultura   54, 96
     Los animales del campo y de la granja   42
     Capdevila, Juan: Nico y Ana en el campo   135
     Puncel, María: Cuando sea mayor trabajaré en una granja   54
     Usborne, Peter and Su Swallow: Huevos   56, 85
     Usborne, Peter and Su Swallow: Leche   58, 85

FARMS--FICTION
     El rabipelado necesario   125

FATHERS--FICTION
     D'Atri, Adriana: Así son papá y mamá   142

FEAR--FICTION
     Bergstrom, Gunilla: ¿Quien te asuuusta Alfonso?   105

FICTION
     Lindgren, Astrid: El tomten   89, 117

FILMS
     Duran, Daniel Flores: Latino materials: a multimedia guide for
          children and young adults   158

FIRE
     Chlad, Dorothy: Cuando hay un incendio sal para afuera   51
     Usborne, Peter, and Su Swallow: Fuego   12, 85

FIREFIGHTERS--FICTION
     Capdevila, Juan: Nico y Ana quieren ser bomberos   135

FIRST AID
     Winch, Brenda: Primeros auxilios   51, 88

FISH
     Van Dulm, Sacha, and Jan Reim: Como vive un pez de río: la
          vida de un espino   45

FISH--FICTION
     Wylie, Joanne and David: Un cuento curioso de colores   156
     Wylie, Joanne and David: Un cuento de un pez grande   156

FISHING--FICTION
Denou, Violeta: Nico y Ana pescadores 112

FLOWERS--FICTION
Zuliani, Fausto: Don Escarabajo tiene un color 156

FOLKLORE (see also FABLES)
Bassile, Giambattista: Petrosinella 19, 89
Belgrano, Margarita: Tío Juan y otros cuentos 66
Bravo-Villasante, Carmen: Advina adivinanza. Folklore infantil 15
Bravo-Villasante, Carmen: Arre moto piti, poto, arre, moto, piti, pa. 15
Bravo-Villasante, Carmen: China, China, Capuchina, en esta mano está la china 15
Ferré, Rosario: Los cuentos de Juan Bobo 21
Garrido, Felipe: Tajín y los sietes truenos 21, 90
Goble, Paul: El don del perro sagrado 22, 90
LaFontaine, Jean de: La tortuga y los dos patos 25, 90
Papp Severo, Emöke de: El bondadoso hermano menor 27, 90

FOLKLORE--ARGENTINA
Garrido de Rodríguez, Neli: Leyendas argentinas 21
Yalí: Las trampas del Curupí y otras leyendas 30

FOLKLORE--CENTRAL AMERICA
Cuentos picarescos para niños de América Latina 20

FOLKLORE--CHILE
Schkolnik, Saul: Cuentos del Tío Juan, el zorro culpeo 29

FOLKLORE--COSTA RICA
Leal de Noguera, María: Cuentos viejos 25
Lyra, Carmen: Cuentos de mi tía Panchita 25

FOLKLORE--ECUADOR
Movischoff Zavala, Paulina: El cóndor de la vertiente: leyenda salasaca 27

FOLKLORE--ENGLAND
Bayley, Nicola: Canciones tontas 14

FOLKLORE--MEXICO
Kurtycz, Marcos, and Ana García Kobeh: De tigres y tlacuaches: leyendas animales 24

FOLKLORE--RUSSIA
Cuentos rusos 20

FOLKLORE--SOUTH AMERICA
Cuentos picarescos para niños de América Latina 20

FOLKLORE--SPAIN
 Jiménez-Landi Martínez, Antonio: Leyendas de España 24

FOLKLORE--PERU
 Jordana Laguna, José Luis: Leyendas amazónicas 24

FOLKLORE--PRE-COLUMBIAN
 Galeano, Eduardo: Aventuras de los jóvenes dioses 21
 Garrido de Rodríguez, Neli: Leyendas argentinas 21
 Movischoff Zavala, Paulina: El cóndor de la vertiente: leyenda
  salasaca 27

FOLKLORE--PUERTO RICO
 Alegría, Ricardo E.: Cuentos folklóricos de Puerto Rico 17
 Belpré, Pura: Oté 19
 Belpré, Pura: Pérez y Martina 19

FOLKLORE--VENEZUELA
 Armellada, Fray Cesáreo de: El cocuyo y la mora 17
 Armellada, Fray Cesáreo de: Panton...(Una mano de los indios
  pemón)
 Armellada, Fray Cesáreo de: El rabipelado burlado 18
 Armellada, Fray Cesáreo de: El tigre y el rayo. Cuento de la
  tribu pemón 19
 Ipuana, Ramón Paz: El conejo y el mapurite 23
 El morrocoy y el llanero 26
 Paz Ipuana, Ramón: El burrito y la tuna 27
 Rivero Oramas, Rafael: La piedra del Zamuro 28
 Uslar Pietri, Arturo: El conuco de tío conejo 29

FOLK MUSIC--PUERTO RICO
 Nieves Falcón, Luis: Mi música 61

FORESTS
 Los animales del bosque y del monte 42
 Saville, Malcolm: El niño quiere saber: explorando un bosque
  56

FORESTS--FICTION
 Cos, Rosa Ma: Historias fantásticas de Ivo y Tino: El bosque
  encantado 109

FOXES--FICTION
 Burningham, John: Harquin el zorro que bajó al valle 106

FRIENDS--FICTION
 Burningham, John: El amigo 134
 D'Atri, Adriana: Así son nuestros amigos 142

FROGS--FICTION
 Chapouton, Anne-Marie: Los Bambalinos y las ranas 138
 Perera, Hilda: Rana ranita 151

FRUIT
  Echeverría, Eugenia: las frutas 55
  Noriega, Luisa de: Yo soy el durazno 55

FRUIT--FICTION
  Lööf, Jan: Historia de una manzana roja 118

GAMES
  Claret, María: Juegos de ayer y de hoy 62
  García Sánchez, José Luis: Los juegos 1 63
  García Sánchez, José Luis: Los juegos 2 63
  García Sánchez, José Luis: Los juegos 3 63
  Graham, Ian: Juegos de computadoras 65, 92
  Schon, Isabel, ed.: Doña Blanca and Other Hispanic Nursery
    Rhymes and Games 17

GARDENING--FICTION
  Turin, Adela: El Jardinero astrólogo 127

GEOGRAPHY
  Von Schweintiz, Dagmar: El niño pregunta: el mar, las montañas
    37

GEOLOGY
  Denou, Violeta: La tierra y sus riquezas 39, 95
  Lambert, David: Actividad de la tierra 36, 94
  Los minerales 36, 96

GEOMETRY--FICTION
  Walsh, María Elena: El país de la geometría 129

GHOSTS--FICTION
  Bergstrom, Gunilla: ¿Quien te asuuusta Alfonso? 105

GIANTS--FICTION
  Company, Mercé: El prisionero del gigante 109

GIRAFFES
  García Sánchez, José Luis, and Miguel Angel Pacheco: La jirafa
    47

GIRLS--FICTION
  Aboites, Luis: El campo y la ciudad 101
  Amo, Montserrat Del: Chitina y su gato 132
  Balzola, Asun: Munia y el cocolilo naranja 132
  Balzola, Asun: Munia y la luna 133
  Balzola, Asun: Munia y la señora Piltronera 132
  Balzola, Asun: Los zapatos de Munia 133
  Barbot, Daniel: Un diente se mueve 134
  Benet, Amelia: Silvia y Miguel en verano 134
  Blume, Judy: La ballena 105

Subject Index
07

GIRLS--FICTION (cont.)
    Blume, Judy: ¿Estás ahí Dios? Soy yo, Margaret 105
    Capdevila, Juan: Nico y Ana en el campo 135
    Capdevila, Juan: Nico y Ana hacen fotos 135
    Capdevila, Juan: Nico y Ana quieren ser bomberos 135
    Capdevila, Juan: Nico y Ana quieren ser médicos 135
    Capdevila, Juan: Nico y Ana quieren ser músicos 135
    Carroll, Lewis: "Alicia" para los niños 89, 106
    Cleary, Beverly: Ramona la chiche 108
    Company, Mercé: ¿Dónde está el tío Ramón? 109
    Company, Mercé: Perdidos en la cueva 109
    D'Atri, Adriana: Así es nuestra casa 140
    D'Atri, Adriana: Así es nuestro perro 140
    D'Atri, Adriana: Así pasamos al día 141
    D'Atri, Adriana: Así Somos nosotros 141
    D'Atri, Adriana: Así son los abueios que viven cerca 141
    D'Atri, Adriana: Así son los abuelos que viven lejos 141
    D'Atri, Adriana: Así son los tíos 142
    D'Atri, Adriana: Así son nuestros amigos 142
    D'Atri, Adriana: Así son papá y mamá 142
    Delgado, Eduardo: Los Mecs cocineros 111
    Delgado, Eduardo: Los Mecs juegan a ser actores 111
    Delgado, Eduardo: Los Mecs juegan en la playa 111
    Delgado, Eduardo: Los Mecs van de excursión 112
    Delgado, Eduardo: Los Mecs van en bicicleta 112
    Denou, Violeta: Nico y Ana pescadores 112
    Ichikawa, Satomi: Susana y Nicolás en el mercado 115
    Kurtz, Carmen: Veva 116
    Lindgren, Astrid: Madita 117
    Llega un hermanito 150
    Llimona, Mercedes: Bibí y el verano 118
    Llimona, Mercedes: Bibí y la primavera 118
    Otero, Rodolfo: Milla Loncó 119
    Oxenbury, Helen: En casa de los abuelos 151
    Paz, Marcela: Papelucho perdido 123
    Posadas Mañé, Carmen de: El señor Viento Norte 123
    Puncel, María: Clara y el caimán 124
    Sola, María Luisa: Ana 126
    Stinson, Kathy: El rojo es el mejor 152
    Thurber, James: Muchas lunas 126
    Turin, Adela: Las cajas de cristal 126
    Vanhalewijn, Mariette: La brujita Wanda 127
    Vanhalewijn, Mariette: Los 365 vestidos de la princesa Penélope
        128
    Vázquez-Vigo, Carmen: Caramelos de menta 128

GOLD PROSPECTING--FICTION
    Alvarez, Agustín S.: Aventuras de loberos 102

GRAMMAR see specific language with the subdivision: e.g.,
    ENGLISH LANGUAGE--GRAMMAR

MYTHOLOGY--CHINA
Sanders, Tao Tao Liu: Dragones, dioses y espíritus de la mitología
china 10

MYTHOLOGY--GREEK
Gibson, Michael: Monstruos, dioses y hombres de la mitología
griega 10

MYTHOLOGY--NORSE
Branston, Brian: Dioses y héroes de la mitología vikinga 10

MYTHOLOGY--ROMAN
Usher, Kerry: Emperadores, dioses y héroes de la mitología romana 10

MYTHOLOGY--SOUTH AMERICA
Gifford, Douglas: Guerreros, dioses y espíritus de la mitología
de América Central y Sudamérica 10

NATURAL HISTORY
El niño pregunta; Las carreras de coches, La fuerza de la naturaleza 3

NATURE
Denou, Violeta: La fuerza de la naturaleza 37, 95
Greé, Alain: Tom e Irene descubren las estaciones 35
Kincaid, Lucy: Mira abajo 31
Kincaid, Lucy: Mira adentro 32
Kincaid, Lucy: Mira alrededor 32
Kincaid, Lucy: Mira arriba 32
Provensen, Alice, and Martin Provensen: El libro de las esta-
ciones 35

NATURE--FICTION
Cos, Rosa Ma: Historias fantásticas de Ivo y Tino: El bosque
encantado 109

NEWSPAPERS
El periódico 100

NIGHT
Solano Flores, Guillermo: La Noche 36, 99

NORTH AMERICA
Los animales de América del Norte 43

NUMBERS--FICTION
Ugalde Alcántara, Felipe: Los números 153

NURSERY RHYMES
Bayley, Nicola: Canciones tontas 14

PARROTS
  Prim, Victor and Helena Ross: El loro busca casa 57, 91

PATAGONIA
  Guait, Camilo: Viaje al país de las manzanas 81

PERU
  Millard, Anne: Los incas 81

PETS (see also specific animals: e.g., CATS, DOGS)
  Puncel, María: Clara y el caimán 124

PETS--FICTION
  D'Atri, Adriana: Así es nuestro perro 140
  Denou, Violeta: Teo y su perro 144
  Denou, Violeta: Los animales de Teo 143
  Hoff, Syd: Danielito y el dinosauro 149
  Oxenbury, Helen: Nuestro perro 151

PHOTOGRAPHY--FICTION
  Capdevila, Juan: Nico y Ana hacen fotos 135
  Vincent, Gabrielle: César y Ernestina van al fotógrafo 155

PHYSICAL FITNESS
  Usborne, Peter, and Su Swallow: Dormir 51, 86

PHYSICS
  La física 36, 96
  Satchwell, John: Como funciona la energía 52, 94

PHYSIOLOGY
  El cuerpo humano 50, 96
  Murphy, Chuck: Tu cuerpo 50
  Murphy, Chuck: Tus sentidos 50
  Rayner, Clare: El libro del cuerpo 50
  Rius, María, J. M. Parramón, J. J. Puig: El gusto 50
  Rius, María, J. M. Parramón, J. J. Puig: La vista 51
  Rius, María, J. M. Parramón, J. J. Puig: El oído 51
  Rius, María, J. M. Parramón, J. J. Puig: El olfacto 51
  Rius, María, J. M. Parramón, J. J. Puig: El tacto 51
  Usborne, Peter and Su Swallow: Dientes 51, 86

PICASSO
  Morán, Francisco José: Pablo Ruiz Picasso 83

PICNICS--FICTION
  Vincent, Gabrielle: César y Ernestina van de picnic 155

PLANES--FICTION
  Capdevila, Juan: Teo en avión 137

220   Basic Collection of Books in Spanish

SATIRE (cont.)
   Cervantes Saavedra, Miguel de: Aventuras de don Quijote de la
   Mancha 73

SCHOOLS--FICTION
   Burningham, John: La escuela 135
   Capdevila, Juan: Teo en la escuela 137
   Hill, Eric: Spot va a la escuela 148

SCIENCE (see also specific sciences: e. g., BIOLOGY, BOTANY,
   PHYSICS)
   Los animales prehistóricos 39, 96
   Los árboles 42, 96
   Catchpole, Clive: Desiertos 40
   Catchpole, Clive: Junglas 40
   Catchpole, Clive: Montañas 40
   Catchpole, Clive: Praderas 40
   Clark, Mary Lou: Dinosaurios 39, 84
   Cobb, Vicki: Experimentos cientificos que se pueden comer 33
   Denou, Violeta: La fuerza de la naturaleza 37, 95
   Denou, Violeta: El mar 37, 95
   Denou, Violeta: La tierra y sus riquesas 39, 95
   Dos cuentos de vida 39
   La física 36, 96
   Ford, Adam: Observando el clima 38, 94
   Frontera: Infinito hacia el 2000 con las nuevas tecnologías 48
   Giron, Nicole: El mar 40
   Greé, Alain: El agua 100
   Lambert, David: Actividad de la tierra 36, 94
   Lewellen, John: La luna, el sol, y las estrellas 34, 84
   Mayoral, María Teresa: El libro del agua y la vida 37, 97
   Los minerales 36, 96
   Neigoff, Anne: Los lugares donde viven las plantas 41
   Neigoff, Anne: Muchas plantas 41
   Neigoff, Anne: Las plantas que necesitamos 41
   Neigoff, Anne: Las plantas y como crecen 41
   Neigoff, Anne: Las plantas y sus semillas 41
   Osman, Tony: El descubrimiento del universo 33, 98
   Pavord, Anna: Botánica recreativa 42, 87
   Peñarroja, Jordi, and Josep M. Bonet: Juega con ... el agua 32
   Peñarroja, Jordi: Juega con ... el aire 32
   Peñarroja, Jordi: Juego con ... el calor 32
   Peñarroja, Jordi: Juego con ... la electricidad y el magnetismo
   32
   Peñarroja, Jordi: Juego con ... la luz 32
   Peñarroja, Jordi: Juego con ... la química 32
   Pérez de Laborda, Alfonso: La astronomía moderna 34
   Pérez de Laborda, Alfonso: La formación del universo 34
   Sabugo Pintor, Angel: El libro del medio ambiente 41, 97
   Satchwell, John: Como funciona la energía 52, 94
   Schkolnick, Saul: Colorín colorado, ovulito fecundado 39

228 Basic Collection of Books in Spanish

TRAINS--RAILROAD see RAILROADS

TRANSPORTATION (see also TRAVEL, RAILROADS, BOATS, SHIPS
AND SAILING, AIRPLANES)
El transporte 13, 96
Usborne, Peter, and Su Swallow: Trenes 13, 86

TRANSPORTATION--HIGHWAY
Greé, Alain: Tom e Irene y el código de circulación 14

TRANSPORTATION--MARINE
Greé, Alain: Yo quiero ser capitán 13
Puncel, María: Cuando sea mayor seré marino 13

TRAVEL--FICTION
Capdevila, Juan: Teo en avión 137
Capdevila, Juan: Teo en barco 137
Capdevila, Juan: Teo en tren 138
Gorostiza, Carlos: El barquito viajero 146
Pacheco, M. A., and J. L. García Sánchez: El viaje de nunca
acabar 120

TREES (see also BOTANY, PLANTS)
Los árboles 42, 96
El niño pregunta: Los animales del zoo; los árboles 3

TUNDRA
Los animales de la tundra y de los hielos 43

TURTLES
La tortuga vuelve a casa 91

UNCLES--FICTION
D'Atri, Adriana: Así son los tíos 142

UNITED STATES
Anno, Mitsumasa: El viaje de Anno IV 80
Krueger, Bonnie, and Martine Steltzer: Vivir en Estados Unidos
80

VACATIONS--FICTION
Paz, Marcela: Papelucho en vacaciones 121

VENEZUELA
Pipo Kilómetro viaja por Venezuela: Primera parte 82
Pipo Kilómetro viaja por Venezuela: Segunda parte 82

VENEZUELA--FICTION
Kurusa: La calle es libre 117

VENTRILOQUISTS--FICTION
Vázquez-Vigo, Carmen: El muñeco de don Bepo 128